BLOOD
AND
FLESH

RECENT TITLES IN CONTRIBUTIONS IN AFRO-AMERICAN AND
AFRICAN STUDIES
SERIES ADVISER: HOLLIS R. LYNCH

Africans and Creeks: From the Colonial Period to the Civil War
Daniel F. Littlefield, Jr.

Decolonization and Dependency: Problems of Development
of African Societies
Aquibou Y. Yansané, editor

The American Slave: A Composite Autobiography
Supplement, Series 2
George P. Rawick, editor

The Second Black Renaissance: Essays in Black Literature
C. W. E. Bigsby

Advice Among Masters: The Ideal in Slave Management in the
Old South
James O. Breeden, editor

Towards African Literary Independence: A Dialogue with
Contemporary African Writers
Phanuel Akubueze Egejuru

The Chickasaw Freedmen: A People Without a Country
Daniel F. Littlefield, Jr.

The African Nexus: Black American Perspectives on the
European Partitioning of Africa
Sylvia M. Jacobs

Freedom and Prejudice: The Legacy of Slavery in the
United States and Brazil
Robert Brent Toplin

The World of Black Singles: Changing Patterns of
Male/Female Relations
Robert Staples

Survival and Progress: The Afro-American Experience
Alex L. Swan

BLOOD AND FLESH

Black American and African Identifications

Josephine Moraa Moikobu

CONTRIBUTIONS IN AFRO-AMERICAN AND AFRICAN STUDIES,
NUMBER 59

GREENWOOD PRESS
Westport, Connecticut • London, England

Library of Congress Cataloging in Publication Data

Moikobu, Josephine Moraa, 1949-
   Blood and flesh.

   (Contributions in Afro-American and African studies ;
no. 59 ISSN 0069-9624)
   Bibliography: p.
   Includes index.
   1. Afro-Americans—Relations with Africans. 2. Afro-
Americans—Race identity. 3. Afro-American college
students—New York (State)—Case studies. 4. African
students in New York (State)—Case studies. I. Title.
II. Series.
E185.615.M59   305.8'96073   80-1706
ISBN 0-313-22549-4 (lib. bdg.)

Library of Congress Catalog Card Number: 80-1706
ISBN: 0-313-22549-4
ISSN: 0069-9624

First published in 1981

Greenwood Press
A division of Congressional Information Service, Inc.
88 Post Road West, Westport, Connecticut 06881

Printed in the United States of America

10 9 8 7 6 5 4 3 2 1

IN MEMORY OF
TOM JOSEPH MBOYA, KWAME NKRUMAH, AND
LULU
AND
DEDICATED TO
MWALIMU JULIUS K. NYERERE,
ALEX HALEY, AND
ANDREW YOUNG

Contents

Tables

Preface

The major purpose of this study is to explore whether or not black Americans and Africans identify with one another. Specifically, the study seeks to uncover the nature, character, and extent of black American and African identification.

Black Americans and Africans have been studied extensively. Frequently, black Americans are studied in relation to white Americans in their society as a whole; similarly Africans are studied in relation to their former European colonial overlords or through self-contained ethnographic studies using a tribal setting as a background. Very few studies have attempted to study black Americans and Africans directly in relation to each other. Those few who have dared to venture into this field of study mostly have concluded that black Americans and Africans have really nothing in common with one another except for color and ancestry, black Americans and Africans do not interact socially, and those who do, more often than not, have "strained" social interactions.

The data presented are derived from four different sources: participant observations, questionnaires, interviews, and extensive library research. My early observations while studying in the United States during the 1960s were not part of this data. However, the impressions I gained then concerning the relationships between black Americans and Africans helped me formulate the basis for my later study. Formal participant observations were conducted during 1971 and 1972 on two campuses of the

State University of New York. The information from questionnaires was obtained from a stratified random sample of two
black populations, consisting of black American and African
students. The entire campus population of more than 150
black American and African students was first identified. From
this number a random sample was drawn of 40 black American
and 40 black African students.

The purpose of this study, it should be stressed, is exploratory
and not to test a hypothesis.

This book would not have been written without the intellectual and emotional support of a number of people. A very special
debt of gratitude is extended first to the respondents, both
black Americans and Africans, for their willingness to participate
in this study.

LaFrances Rogers-Rose is thanked particularly for her
patient guidance in the drafting, analysis, and writing phases
of the research. It is hoped that this book is worthy of the
intellectual stimulation that she provided continuously and un-
selfishly on numerous occasions. Benjamin Bowser, dean,
Cornell University, whose enlightened and meticulous criticisms and constant encouragement paved the way for the successful completion of this work, is thanked particularly. Terrence
K. Hopkins also provided a strong theoretical and methodological hand throughout this study, without which this study
would not have progressed. His often critical advice and guidance provided me with the new perspective in which the study
is anchored, and to him my utmost gratitude is extended.

The author would also like to take this occasion formally
to recognize several persons who have been instrumental
throughout her long academic career. Without their emotional
support and encouragement, this book would not have been
realized. All members of my family are to be thanked especially
for their willingness to tolerate the long absence from home
necessitated by the many years of my formal academic train-
ing in the United States. Fred G. Burke, the New Jersey state
commissioner of education, is given special recognition for his
appreciation and deep understanding of the particular problems often experienced by homesick foreign students studying

in the United States. Arlene Poreda, is thanked for typing the final manuscript. Finally, the present study is a personal tribute to the memory of Thomas Joseph Mboya, former minister of economic planning and development in the Kenyan government. Dr. Mboya is thanked especially for his initial advice, guidance, and suggestions urging me to pursue my higher education abroad. Therefore, the subject matter covered in this book stems in part from Dr. Mboya's hopes and dreams that unity and harmony would someday prevail among black peoples and others throughout the world. It is hoped that this book contributes in some way, however small, to this worthy goal. Any flaws in this book are my sole responsibility.

BLOOD
AND
FLESH

Introduction

The purpose of this study was to explore whether or not black Americans and Africans identify with one another. Specifically, the study sought to uncover the nature, character, and extent of black American and African identifications.

This study came about when as a black African, I had an opportunity to pursue my education in the United States. Arriving in the United States, I carried with me some rudimentary knowledge about some Africans who, a long time ago, had been forcefully torn from their homeland and carried off as slaves to many parts of the world, including the United States where their descendants still live. With this knowledge, I hoped to learn more about these supposedly displaced Africans and to learn of their association (if any) with Africa and other Africans.

On arrival at an American campus, I quickly learned there were no black American students, or even Africans. I found myself the only black or African specimen in the midst of a sea of whites. It was not until several campuses later that I finally managed to meet some African students. Here too, I soon learned, African students associated with one another, other foreign students, and with white Americans. We African students lived isolated from the black American students on campus, as well as from the larger black community just outside the campus. In particular, we were insulated from events occurring in the black community beyond the confines of the university campus. The few black American students at the university rarely associated with Africans, or the Africans with them. Some of the curiosity that African students displayed at times about the American "Negroes" were met by whites with such comments as: "You have really nothing in common with 'those Negroes,' " or "They really don't like or want you." Myths and stereotypes that accompanied these remarks were often adequately enumerated to accentuate the differences that were strongly felt to exist between the "you" (African students) and "them" (American Negroes). The black students (Africans and black Americans) appeared unaware of the degree of accuracy of the supposedly unbreachable differences said to exist between them. As no effort was made to interact socially with each other, the students lived in mutually blissful ignorance of each other. The African students lived and studied in an academically protected sanctuary, while the black Americans lived somewhere very close to the university but, nevertheless, separately. The fact that these two groups of students lived so close and yet so far away from each other and the presumed notion that they did not have much in common bothered me.

During the mid-1960s several major events took place that seemed to shake American institutions to their very foundations: the Civil Rights Movement, student unrest, and the racial disorders that set American cities ablaze throughout the nation. The racial issue seemed to come to the forefront, and most of the African students who had been living within the protective confines of the university could no longer ignore racial matters as if they did not directly or indirectly concern us. It was a time when historical events and real-life contradictions forced most of us to reconsider our place in that terribly confusing world. In effect, we had to choose. Unlike earlier, we could no longer remain complacent, hiding behind our own comfortable, though precarious, diverse masks of exotic foreign nationalities. The choice that some of us had to make was not limited to ethical and moral concerns, but rather challenged the very core of our being. For me, one result of this challenge was actively to wonder and seek to understand African

Americans. For most of us Africans, having to deny the social realities all around us would have been a denial of our very selves, as well as our African heritage and whatever else we as a people represented. Questions arose about our history and, above all, our common ancestral origins that inextricably linked us (recent Africans) and those African descendants in the New World—our flesh and blood.

In the early 1960s a black face on an all-white campus was, more often than not, either a black African or a West Indian. I left the United States for Africa in the late 1960s. But when I returned in the early 1970s, I discovered the social turbulance of the 1960s had passed and the process of metamorphosis appeared to allow an increase of black American students on most white campuses. This was coupled with a considerable shrinkage of the African student population. In contrast to the 1960s, African students had begun associating much more with black Americans and somewhat less with American whites. This seemed to contradict what I had observed and learned earlier. Looking for answers, I surveyed the literature that dealt with black American and African relationships. In the process, I discovered there was hardly any empirical information dealing directly with black American and African relationships. However, there was a plethora of data in many fields that seemed to deal with blacks in relation to whites both in Africa and in the United States. Also, most studies that touched upon any aspect of black American and African relations seemed to indicate that black Americans and Africans do not really have much in common with one another except their ancestry and color. Whatever relationships were found to exist were, more often than not, characterized as "strained." This change of associational patterns that I noted and the contradictory impressions from my literature survey raised fundamental questions that begged for answers: Did this associational change come as a result of changes within the larger social, political, and economic environment? Did the new status of Africa in the international community affect African-American relations? What was the nature and extent of these relations? Did black Americans and Africans identify with each other? If so, then what were some of the most important dimensions of their perceived common identifications? And if so, what was the nature and extent of black social interactions? What was the basis of social strains? Were the perceived social strains due to the two black groups or were strains perceived to come from somewhere outside these two black groups?

To answer these questions, the present study was initiated during the academic year 1971 to 1972 in one large metropolitan area in New York state. The metropolitan area was chosen because it represented a cross section of the target population needed for this study. The area included a cross section that was representative of the larger national black American community. Because of the presence of one large State University of New York campus and several other smaller institutions of higher learning nearby, there were also a number of African students living and studying in this metropolitan area. Therefore, it was felt that studying black relations within this context represented a cross section of black students, both Americans and Africans.

Before beginning my explorations, I surveyed the literature that dealt specifically or generally with black American and African relations. There appeared to be two conflicting impressions that partly paralleled the transformation in African-Afro-American relations.

The first major impression is that which I call the "Eurocentric view." The Eurocentric view of black American and African relations has several distinctive features. Those who express this view maintain that (1) Black Americans and Africans do not in general have much in common with each other except their ancestry and color. (2) Black Americans do not have distinctive social-cultural creations of their own; black people as a group have not contributed much to the larger world civilization.[1] (3) In general, black Americans and Africans do not get along and hence do not closely identify with one another. (4) Among those black Americans and Africans who attempt to interact socially, social relationships are to a large extent characterized as "strained."[2]

However, this premise ran into difficulties when it was discovered that some black life had distinctive social-cultural patterns that did not fit comfortably within the mainstream of American life. These social-cultural peculiarities then acquired different labels. For example, Myrdal characterized the differences as "pathological" and Frazier as "disorganization" and "immorality." Black Americans as a people were called "white men with Black skins,"[3] while to Moynihan and Glazer they turned into "Americans and nothing else." This perception tended to see black Americans only within the American context, without regard to black American cultural origins in Africa. Finally, this Eurocentric view is characterized by its recognition only of black American and African "differences" rather than "similarities" and its emphasis upon perceived social "strains" rather than a full picture that also includes "harmonies." As the Eurocentric view seems to emphasize one aspect of black American and African relations, the strains, the Eurocentric view often fails to see the total picture. If this view examined similarities as well as diversities, a more balanced picture would be provided.

The second major perception is labeled as the "Afrocentric view." The Afrocentric view, like the Eurocentric view, maintains that blacks as a people share one of the most important links known to mankind, flesh and blood, through their common ancestral origins and hence color. As blacks are inextricably linked through their common heritage and history, they have a lot in common, for example, oppression and suppression.[4]

Unlike the Eurocentric view of black relationships, the Afrocentric view places great emphasis on the existence of distinctive and common cultural expressions such as music, dance, and folk tales.[5] Unlike the Eurocentric view, which traces the origins of black Americans to urban ghettoes in the North or slavery in the South, the Afrocentric perspective traces distinctive black American social-cultural patterns to their rightful origins, the larger continent of Africa.[6]

The Afrocentric perspective indicates that black American and African relations as characterized in the 1970s are not by any means new.[7] Rather, they have existed throughout time. The threads of black American and African identification have

been manifested primarily through black arts.[8] Though the
Afrocentric view has a long tradition rooted in black arts, it
has not been expressed fully in the more Eurocentric social
sciences.

The problems inherent in the study of black American and
African relations are complex and deserve close scrutiny. First,
good social scientific information that directly relates to the
relationship of these two groups seems to be lacking. Second,
the few strands that seem to shed some light on black relations
are studied in relation to whites. Because black Americans are
studied within the white American framework, their distinctive
social-cultural creations and characteristics, which do not seem
to fit comfortably within the larger mainstream of American
culture, come to be viewed and interpreted as "deviant" or
"pathological." Social scientists identified as representing the
Eurocentric view include Moynihan, Glazer, Myrdal, Stampp,
and Frazier, to name just a few. (The Eurocentric view will be
dealt with in detail in Chapter 1.) These scholars studied various
aspects of black American life, but they failed to track and
trace distinctive black American characteristics to their rightful
origins—the continent of Africa.

Those social scientists opposed to this view include Melville
Herskovits, who not only discovered African survivals within
the black American community but also went a step further:
he traced them through the islands and finally to Africa.[9]

Like Herskovits, Billingsley[10] and Blauner[11] have more recently asserted that in spite of the cruel institution of slavery
that supposedly wiped out all black America's African survivals
within the black community, the black American community
still does have its own distinctive past, and its distinctive cultural
characteristics still survive in America. James E. Blackwell
(1975)[12] stated that "much of what has survived originated in
the African past." According to Blackwell, African survivals as
characterized within the larger black American community
include: "family patterns and attitudes, songs, dance, religious
practices, superstition, ways of walking, verbal expressions,
music, given names for children, and traditional foods."[13]
Blauner and others[14] have proposed that "an authentic Black

culture survived slaves and it is to be found today largely in the urban ghettoes of Black America." Blackwell stresses further that this same black culture has its roots in the parallel institutions that evolved and crystallized social relationships among the members of the black community.[15]

In comparison to the Eurocentric approach, which argues the "lack of relations" and "strains" inherent in black American and African relations, the Afrocentric perspective holds that there is no human social situation where social relationships are all "positive." For instance, the relationships that exist between husbands and their wives, parents and their children, or among siblings are also sometimes characterized by "strain." The fact that most human relations are characterized by strain does not necessarily dismiss whatever bonds may exist. If this fact is generally accepted, the Afrocentric perspective argues further, why then are bonds that exist among blacks denied? To answer this question, increasing numbers of blacks, both Africans and Americans, emphasize the "existence" of bonds and hence an identification with one another that goes far and beyond those of ancestry and color per se. They stress harmony rather than disharmony, lack of strain rather than presence of strain, in black American and African relations, where they emphasize identification.

The information used throughout this study was obtained from four different sources: participant observation, questionnaires, interviews, and library research.

The information resulting from the questionnaires was obtained from a stratified random sample of two black populations consisting of black American and African students. The researcher identified the entire population of more than 150 black American and African students on campus. From this number a random sample was made of 40 black American and 40 black African students on campus. After the roster was obtained, the researcher copied the name of each student on a separate piece of paper. Each batch of names was placed in a basket and mixed, and names were drawn randomly with the help of two black assistants. It is likely that there were more than 200 black students on campus. Of these, the majority

were accessible to the researcher. Black students in the natural
sciences who did not participate in Afro-American programs
on campus might have been missed, but those missed were
probably so few in number that their unintended exclusion
did not significantly alter the nature of this study.

It should be stressed again that the core of this study was
exploratory. It was considered essential first to explore the
field of black relations, which afforded me the methodological
flexibility to delve into this important area, long ignored by
social scientists. Also, it would be impossible to test yet-unde-
fined insights about a topic that has never been studied before.

Throughout the study I immersed myself in the everyday
lives of both black communities to get ideas for future analysis.
Participant observation was conducted by attendance at both
formal and informal social situations that involved both groups
of black students. Much valuable contextual information was
collected this way. After a period of four months of intensive
participant observation, it was decided to supplement participant observation with a social survey of the aforementioned
sample and through formal interviews.

This exploratory study set out to investigate the relations
between a small number of black American and African college
and university students. It also attempted to discover the
nature of the students' perceptions of their social interactions.
By deepening and sensitizing these perceptions, it hoped to
throw light and attention upon problems felt to exist between
the two black groups. It also attempted to discover, identify,
and analyze some of the social interaction patterns that existed
or were thought to have existed among black Americans and
Africans.

In order to gain insight into the study and to interpret the
results of my field notes and questionnaires, it is necessary to
review the related literature in Chapters 1 through 4. Chapter 1
examines the Eurocentric perspective of black relations. Information based upon the work of social scientists who seem to
support this view and empirical studies and information that
form "journalistic impressions" are all presented to give a
better understanding of black relations from a Eurocentric

viewpoint. Chapter 2 presents an Afrocentric view of black relations. Political movements such as Garvey's Universal Negro Improvement Association, Du Bois' Pan-African Movement, and the Colonization Society, which attempted to bring back black people together in their own diverse ways, are studied. In Chapter 3 the Afrocentric view is examined through black people's informal movements represented in black literature. Chapter 4 presents an analysis and interpretation of data from 80 black American and African students on an American campus to discover the latest views concerning black identity and relationships: what items the students felt they had in common with one another, as dimensions of black peoples' identity, consisting of those things that both groups like most about each other as well as common identifications. Chapter 5 deals with what the students perceived to be their own black social relationships. In Chapter 6 both groups' perceptions of their social interactions with whites are probed further. Though this study, it should be stressed, is intended to focus specifically on black social relationships, it was discovered that black-white relationships kept creeping in. The black-white relationships dealt with here are presented from a black point of view. Chapter 7 discusses black American and African male-female relationships. White females' infiltration into black male-female relationships ranked high. The conclusion summarizes the findings of this study and provides concluding remarks.

The Eurocentric, Afrocentric, political, and informal analyses are interrelated as each chapter, in its own way, examines the black relationships. Looking at each component will give us a better understanding of black relations. The information gathered will aid in the interpretation of my own data.

This study explores whether or not and in what ways black Americans and Africans identify with each other. The study demonstrates specific dimensions in the relationships between the two groups. It also probes into new areas, delineating crucial links that unite them. For example, it considers feelings of "oppression" and "suppression" that can transcend matters of color and ancestry. It also investigates the two groups' social interaction patterns as they perceive their relations with one

another and with the white community. More important, the
issue of social strains felt to exist between these two groups is
explored. The social relationship profile that emerges between
black American and African identifications, in the end, provides
us with a better understanding of the nature, extent, and
character of black American and African social relationships
and identifications.

Notes

1. Gunnar Myrdal, *An American Dilemma: The Negro Problem and
Modern Democracy* (New York: Harper and Brothers, 1944); Nathan
Glazer and Daniel Patrick Moynihan, *Beyond the Melting Pot* (Cam-
bridge, Mass.: M.I.T. and Harvard University Press, 1963); Kenneth M.
Stampp, *The Peculiar Institution: Slavery in Ante-Bellum South* (New
York: Alfred A. Knopf, 1956); E. Franklin Frazier, *The Negro Family
in the United States* (Chicago: The University of Chicago Press, 1966).

2. James M. Davis, Russel G. Hanson, and Duane R. Burnor, *IIE Sur-
vey of the African Student: His Achievements and His Problems* (New York:
International Institute of Education, 1961); Jane W. Jacqz, *African Students
at U.S. Universities* (New York: African American Institute [AAI], 1967);
A. David John, ed., *Africa as Seen by American Negroes* (New York:
American Society of African Cultures, 1958).

3. Stampp, 1956, p. vii.

4. W. E. B. Du Bois, *The World and Africa* (New York: International
Publishers, 1946); Kwame Nkrumah, *The African Background Outlined:
Handbook for the Study of the Negro* (Washington, D.C.: The Associa-
tion for the Study of Negro Life and History, Inc., 1936); Elliot P.
Skinner, *Afro-Americans and Africa: The Continuing Dialectic* (New
York: Columbia University, 1973).

5. Charles A. Valentine, *Black Studies and Anthropology: Scholarly
and Political Interests in Afro-American Culture* (Reading, Mass.: Addison-
Wesley Modular Publications 15, 1972).

6. Melville J. Herskovits, "What Has Africa Given America?" *New
Republic* 1083:92-94; Norman E. Whitten and John F. Szwed, eds.,
Afro-American Anthropology: Contemporary Perspectives (New York:
Macmillan Press, 1970a).

7. George Shepperson, "Notes on Negro American Influences on the
Emergence of African Nationalism," *Journal of African History* 1 (1960):
299-312.

8. Gayle Addison, Jr., ed., *The Black Aesthetic* (New York: Doubleday and Company Inc., 1971); William Couch, Jr., ed., *New Black Playwrights: An Anthology* (Baton Rouge: Louisiana State University Press, 1968).

9. Melville J. Herskovits, *The Myth of the Negro Past* (New York: Harper and Brothers, 1941).

10. Andrew Billingsley, *Black Families in White America* (Englewood Cliffs, N.J.: Prentice-Hall, 1968), chap. 1.

11. Robert Blauner, "Black Culture: Myth or Reality." In *Afro-American Anthropology*, ed. Norman Whitten and John Szwed (New York: Doubleday, 1970), chap. 19.

12. James E. Blackwell, *The Black Community: Diversity and Unity* (New York: Dodd, Mead and Company, 1975).

13. Ibid., p. 10.

14. Ibid.

15. Ibid.

1.
Eurocentric View

This chapter examines the Eurocentric view of black social relationships and identifications. The Eurocentric view maintains that black Americans and Africans have little in common with one another except their ancestry and color.

At the core of this premise rests the belief that a black American culture with roots in Africa does not exist. Whatever social-cultural patterns black Americans reflect are attributed to the larger American society, which is predominantly white and European. Any social or cultural patterns that do not seem to fit comfortably within the larger framework of Western civilization are shifted and explained away through the black American slave experience in the southern part of the United States or urban ghetto experience in the North.[1]

In this chapter, three essential elements characteristic of the Eurocentric view will be discussed. First, literature by several social scientists who best characterize this view will be examined. Second, empirical studies from various sources that deal directly with black American and African students in the United States, which span a period of about two decades, will be studied. They point out that black American and African students do not generally interact with one another and hence do not identify with each other. These studies show the extent of strain in these groups' social relationships. Finally, accounts from nonscholars, termed "journalistic impressions," will be reviewed.

The Eurocentric view is a multidimensional one. For instance, a few white scholars from a Eurocentric academic milieu have risen above a Eurocentric academic background and have managed to view black life more accurately. They have adopted and embraced an Afrocentric view of black relationships. For example, Charles A. Valentine, Melville Herskovits, and Richard B. Moore, to name just a few, seem to have captured and embodied the real objective black world. To study a social phenomenon, one has to adopt an appropriate attitude; and these scholars (we shall deal with the Afrocentric view in detail in Chapter 2) have managed to take an Afrocentric attitude toward the study of black life.

Social Scientist Interpretations

Among the social scientists who represent the Eurocentric view of black relations is Gunnar Myrdal. In his classic book, *The American Dilemma* (1944), Myrdal characterized the black American as "an exaggerated American" and concluded that black Americans' community values were "pathological."[2] Of interest to this thesis is a chapter headed "The Negro Community as a Pathological Form of an American Community," in which he concluded: "American Negro culture is not independent of general American culture. It is a distorted development, or a pathological condition of the general American culture."[3]

It is interesting to note that the same black American social-cultural elements the Afrocentric view celebrates as distinctive black American social-cultural survivals are those that Myrdal finds "pathological," including "the instability of the Negro family," "emotionalism in the Negro Church," and "superstition," to name just a few.

Myrdal was, characteristically, studying the "Negro Problem" from a Eurocentric point of view, that is, basically viewing the United States as an "open society." He assumed that as time went by and if desegregation laws were passed and took effect, blacks like other ethnic groups could rise through the ranks of the American social class structure. For blacks collectively this did not happen. What Myrdal overlooked was that the American ideology of an open social class structure is quite different from the activities of class and racial stratification. There is a caste system based upon race.

Carl Degler, a historian reacting to Myrdal's thesis, retorted that Myrdal "falls back upon an essentially class definition of race prejudice" and added, "to make race prejudice principally class prejudice is to lose the insight into reality that is implied in concepts like caste or colour prejudice."[4]

Along this vein, Nathan Glazer and Daniel Patrick Moynihan in their book, *Beyond the Melting Pot* (1963), characterized black Americans thus:

> It is not possible for the Negroes to view themselves as other ethnic groups viewed themselves because—and this is the key to much in the Negro world—the Negro is only an American and nothing else. *He has no values and culture to guard and protect.*[5] [emphasis added]

It is interesting to note that in the second revision of the book (1970), the authors softened their remarks after strong reactions from the black community across the country over the authors' denial of black ethnicity, culture, and values. They indicated that they did not mean what they had written earlier and in turn shifted the blame to "authoritative scholars, among them, E. Franklin Frazier." Realizing their mistake, they finally took heart and admitted that they had indeed ignored "African survivals" and gave credit to "Afro-American and Black Studies" for opening their eyes. Though they realized this important omission, one is still left with a feeling that these scholars were not completely persuaded. For, rather than taking up the issues to fill the gaps of "African cultural survivals" among black Americans by tracking and tracing them to their rightful origins, the continent of Africa, they still insisted that "out of American origins, one can create a distinctive subculture. . . . This has certainly happened as a result of 300 years of Black-American history, and could serve as a sufficient basis for strong organization, regardless of the contribution of African origins."[6]

E. Franklin Frazier, an outstanding black American social

scientist, joined ranks with those whites who held a Eurocentric
view of black Americans, that is, Myrdal, Glazer, and Moynihan.
In his attempts to counteract Herskovits' assertion that some
black American cultural patterns in the United States have their
origins in Africa, Frazier had this to say:

> . . . although the Negro is distinguished from other minor-
> ities by physical characteristics, unlike other racial or
> cultural minorities the Negro is not distinguished by cul-
> ture from the dominant group. Having completely lost
> his ancestral culture, he speaks the same language, prac-
> tices the same religion, and accepts the same values and
> political ideas as the dominant group. Consequently, when
> he speaks of Negro culture in the United States, one can
> only refer to the folk culture of the rural southern Negro
> or the traditional forms of behaviour and values which
> have grown out of the Negro's social and mental isolation.
> Moreover, many of the elements of the Negro culture
> which have grown out of his peculiar experience in Ameri-
> can, such as music, have become part of the general
> American culture.[7]

In Frazier's discussion of the degradation of urban ghetto
blacks and their social life, he characteristically drew a Eurocentric profile of what blacks and their communities had finally
evolved into: "from which practically all institutional life has
disappeared," where "families are losing their internal cohe-
sion" and "being freed from the controlling force of public
opinion." Black existence, he said, was characterized by "personal demoralization" and sexually "the restrictions which once
held in check immoral conduct lose their force."[8]

Though Frazier in his analysis saw some of the black Americans' social and cultural patterns as "primitive," he nonetheless did not trace them back to their origin in Africa. However,
he prematurely placed them within the decadent northern urban
ghettoes and their birthplace in southern slave plantations.
Though he attributed this background to black people and
their culture, he applied a Eurocentric yardstick to measure and

characterize blacks and their social-cultural institutions. Against this background, he discovered that black family life was a "waste of human life, immorality, delinquency, desertions, and broken homes." This is the result, he concluded, of "the inevitable consequences of that attempt of a pre-literate people, stripped of their cultural heritage, to adjust themselves to civilization."[9]

Implicit in these statements is the conclusion that an attempt by blacks to recoup their dignity and human rights by looking into their past would be a futile exercise. But Frazier had a way out. He gave blacks credit for having managed thus far to "survive in a civilization based upon laissez-faire and competition." He also described blacks as "taking on folkways and mores of the white race." Hence, "the Negro has found within the patterns of White man's culture a purpose in life and a significance for his striving."[10] Evidently a logical conclusion is that if it had not been for the white man's culture, black people in America would not have had a purpose in life. Frazier states further:

> Since the institutions, the social stratification, and the culture of the Negro minority are essentially the same as those of the larger community, it is not strange that the Negro minority belongs among the assimilationist rather than the pluralist, secessionist, or militant minorities. *It is seldom that one finds Negroes who think of themselves as possessing a different culture from whites and their peculiar culture should be preserved.*[11] [emphasis added]

It is not surprising that Frazier concludes as do Glazer and Moynihan that black Americans have a peculiar culture to be preserved. It is a Eurocentric view originating from a Western tradition of scholarship.

Other scholars such as Michael Harrington (1962) shifted focus from the concept of the black family's disorganization and placed it in its proper perspective by suggesting that cultural poverty was directly related to black needs for employment, education, and voting rights.[12]

Perhaps one of the most vehement critics of Frazier is Charles
A. Valentine. Valentine criticized Frazier's conception of the
disintegration of black folks' culture under the impact of urbanization, which was based on data obtained from the census,
other statistical reports, social agencies' reports, and case
histories from social workers. Valentine concluded that:

> An essential element in Frazier's reasoning is one that is
> perpetuated by later thinkers. This is a direct logical leap
> from social statistics, which are deviant in terms of middle-
> class norms, to a model of disorder and instability. Such
> reasoning effectively eliminates consideration of possible
> cultural forms that, in spite of differing from Frazier's
> assumed standard, might have their own order and func-
> tion.[13]

Later in the 1960s trends in sociological studies shifted somewhat from macro-to microsociology, which brought about much
closer observation, often with a touch of empathy. Some sociologists took a bolder step toward a better understanding of
their subjects.

McWorter (1969) criticized Frazier's assimilationist stand
that seemed to suggest the black family should conform to the
white middle-class family.[14] On black Americans' supposedly
matriarchal families, Jackson (1969) joined to criticize the concept of black matriarchy, with disfunctional households, as well
as the division of labor.[15] Elliot Liebow (1960) studied a group
of black men.[16]

Glasco and Gutman (1976) studied blacks in Buffalo, New
York, but they did not find the black "pathology" that Frazier
and others had talked about.[17] They conducted another study
with a group comparable to that studied by Moynihan and
Glazer. Here, too, they did not find a "tangle of pathology."

We shall now turn to examine some empirical studies that
deal directly with the relationships between black Americans
and African students in the United States, to see how such relationships are characterized.

Supportive Empirical Studies

Davis, Hansen and Burnor (1961) conducted a study of 1,010 Africans studying in the United States in 1961-1962, on behalf of the Institute of International Education.[18] They pointed out that, in general, black Americans and Africans do not interact socially as well as they perhaps should and had this to say: "[They] believed that American Negroes and Africans had difficulty getting along. A minority of 23% of African students interviewed stated that in their opinion, Africans and American Negroes got along well together."[19] However, of all those African students who felt that they did not get along well with American blacks, the study made a further breakdown indicating that "Of the 63% who reported problems, 13% indicated that they sometimes don't get along; 40% stated that they had not enough contact to judge or they just did not answer the questions."[20] The study also pointed out that "A few students said they had been given an opportunity to meet Negro families during the orientation period but in most cases, only White families had provided them home hospitality."[21]

Livingston's study of African students in the United States also pointed out the social strain between Africans and black Americans. He wrote:

> The contact between African and American Negro students has oftentimes been unhappy. The Negro undergraduate does not generally share the interest in Africans or the attachment to Africa felt by his college president or some of his deans and professors. The African is met by attitudes ranging from student apathy to open hostility; he is put off by the anti-intellectualism and poor study habits around him.[22]

Logan (1958) asked forty students in his class at Howard University to give their views of Africa.[23] He discovered that many of his students had heard the usual stereotypes of Africa: "the dark continent," "the mysterious continent." Africa was "hot"; it had no civilization of its own; it was inhabited by cannibals, heathens, and ferocious animals living in impenetrable jungles. One student who had even had a course in African history indicated that "she saw no special reason for being interested in Africa." Professor Logan also observed contradictions in his students:

> The most common reasons given by the 63% who indicated some degree of difficulty were a) that American Negroes were unfriendly toward Africans (19%), and b) that American Negroes acted superior (13%). Other reasons cited were the superiority feelings of both groups.[24]

This study also recognized the complexity of African and black American relationships by pointing out that 15% of the African students interviewed had indicated that they did not have any black American friends, while the Africans who had varying numbers of black friends still indicated difficulties in the relationship between the two groups. These difficulties were summed up by an African undergraduate from a small midwestern college who said:

> I personally don't understand American Negroes, and I think American Negroes fail to understand Africans. Africans have been brought up in one culture, and American Negroes are victims of circumstances in another culture and don't know where they belong.[25]

When the same study inquired into the black African students' preferences, whether they would prefer to be with black or white students, most of them registered no preferences at all (82.5%). They indicated the need to meet both groups equally, which is significant in its own right. Most people assume that, because Africans do socially interact with members of both groups or do have more white friends, Africans prefer whites to blacks. However, what is most revealing concerning the reasons why Africans tend to have more whites as friends than blacks was seen in the following statement by one of the African students. He said, "The International Center only arranges for us to meet whites." Some of them said, "My home is not here. My home is in Africa. I want to go home to my people." Another said, "The American Negro is forgetting his African heritage." The professor noted, "Those who are forgetting their African heritage are proud of their light color; those who cling to their African heritage boast of their black skins."[26]

Veroff (1963) investigated whether African students' attitudes toward Americans changed or remained the same as those they held before their experience in the United States.[27] If they changed, in which direction? In comparing students who had spent some time in the United States with those who had just arrived, interesting patterns emerged:

> There are appraisals of Americans that do not seem to be conditioned by how long African students stay here. There are things about Americans that are as apparent immediately as they are two years later: on the positive side, our friendliness and our industriousness; and, on the negative side, our intolerance of foreigners and Negroes in this country, such intolerance mentioned by forty-three percent of African students.[28]

According to a study conducted by the United States Advisory Commission on International Education and Cultural Affairs (1966),[29] and another study by Howard University on Attitudes and Interests of Foreign Students (1965),[30] more often than not African students did not get along well with black Americans. Both of these studies were concerned with attitudes of foreign students toward the United States. Both studies indicated that African students more than other foreign students said that they lived with and had friends among other African students. Also, this group said that they were "without friends" and had the least number of friends among Americans. They described other American students as "less friendly than expected." The Howard study indicated that many African students found the Howard student body "indifferent" (21.9 percent), while others (7.3 percent) characterized them as

"very unfriendly." Twenty-two percent indicated that they
had never visited the home of an American student.

The commission found some African students who felt "very
isolated and homesick," while 25 percent found "no sympathetic or understanding persons" at their university. Another
25 percent felt "alone," and 20 percent said they were homesick "many times."

Other foreign students were found to have difficulties similar
to those of African students, though less pervasive.

Perhaps one of the most exhaustive studies examining the
foreign students' attitudes toward America and Americans was
that of Morris (1960).[31] Comparing white and nonwhite
foreign students, the study discovered that the non-European
students (Asians, Middle-Easterners, Latin Americans, and
Africans) overwhelmingly felt that the depth of personal relationships, equal opportunities for racial and religious groups,
and frequency of undemocratic practices in the United States
were important items. Both white and nonwhite groups felt
that personal relations were deep at home but shallow in
America. Both groups agreed that equality for minority groups
is less here than at home, and both were inclined to dislike the
situation here. Both agreed that undemocratic practices occur
more here than at home and disliked this feature of American
life. The significant difference is that the non-Europeans consider these items more important in determining their overall
attitudes toward this country than do the Europeans.

Both groups of students expressed favorable and unfavorable
attitudes towards the United States. It was important also that
this study highlighted the role of foreign students in a foreign
land. They have to adjust in many facets of life—their academic
life, their social life, the way the Americans view them and
their country, and other related matters.

Another study conducted by the University of California at
Los Angeles (1968) by Halston also indicated that African students' relationships with black American students are less
friendly.[32] This study only investigated African students' attitudes toward American blacks. African students were very critical of their brothers and sisters in the United States. They
clearly indicated that they did not have many blacks as personal

friends. They preferred whites to blacks as personal friends, because of their higher level of educational attainment. Whites were characterized as more understanding, more widely read, and knowledgeable about national and international matters of interest to African students. The Africans indicated that communication with black Americans was difficult. The study also indicated that Africans were accorded preferential treatment by whites:

> Our data tend to support this reasoning; they attest to the fact that African students both aspired to and were accorded an identity distinct from that of black Americans, an identity that conferred higher status and greater acceptance by the white majority, but one which required constant reaffirmation because of its inherent precariousness. The interview materials leave no doubt that our African respondents were very much aware of their relatively advantageous position *vis-à-vis* black Americans, a fact that complicated their relations with blacks and gave rise to "ideological indigestion" of varying degrees of severity among Africans.[33]

On the question of black Americans' identification with Africa, one of the respondents had the following to say:

> Negro identification with Africa is imaginary, like Americans identifying with European countries. Having the same color does not make for common identification. For the first time the American Negro feels related to Africa. But the American Negro will never fit into African society. In Africa he will be treated as an American unless he proves himself. Many American Negroes were rejected in Africa. Some American Negroes don't want to identify with "wild" Africa; you cannot tear yourself from your country. Some of the African students want to encourage that, but they should recognize the frustrations. Thus American Negroes have a different value system. They have a different view point. Their problems must be solved here.[34]

Journalistic Impressions

Perhaps some of the most negative assertions concerning strained relationships between Africans and American blacks were those provided by journalistic impressions—"journalistic" in that the authors spent a relatively short time travelling in Africa, and what they perceived to be "strained" relationships between these groups made up the bulk of their reports. These reports were not based upon precise and systematic scientific investigations.

For example, Harold Isaacs (1961) in his article "Back to Africa" points out that he had travelled to West Africa "to observe among other things, some of the interactions between world politics and race relations."[35] His special inquiry took him to four West African countries: Nigeria, Ghana, Guinea, and Liberia. On his trip he pointed out that he talked to Negroes concerning "impersonal," as well as "personal," matters.

Isaacs tells of having met a black American specialist in a certain West African country who had related to him that he had gone to Africa to look for a comfortable place. "I thought I might feel more free, just settle down and do a job and be myself." The black American answered Isaacs' unasked question: "No, I haven't."

Isaacs stated:

> Practically all the American Negroes I met in West Africa had come to the ancestral continent with some of the same idea in their minds. They had come looking for freedom from racism and prejudice, or at least for a racial situation that counted them in instead of out, that provided solace and a sense of identity in a world where everyone was black. They had also looked for a chance to share in the new pride of achievement stemming from the black man's reassertion of himself and his African personality.[36]

Some questions one is led to ask concerning the black American search for freedom from racism and prejudice or the need to be counted "in" rather than "out" is: Can racism and racial prejudice exist between members of the same race? Or is this a semantic confusion? Does racial unity alone provide unity in all areas of social life? Do black Americans in Africa feel alienated, "left out," because they are black, or is it because they are also Americans?

Certainly, empirical evidence from the continent of Africa or any other social situation does not support Isaacs' implied unity based upon racial dimension. Tribal bloodshed in Africa itself has often involved people of the same color.

Isaacs points out that the Negroes' enchantment with Africa often does not last long—hardly past the first flush of the sensation of being in a place where the white man is not master. Almost invariably, the Negro pilgrim to Africa soon finds himself not free at all, more than ever without solace and a sense of identity, fighting new patterns of prejudice, and suffering the pangs of a new kind of "outsideness."[37]

Are these patterns of prejudice new and unusual only to black Americans in Africa? Or is it a common feeling of any geographically removed people returning to their ancestral homes for the first time? How do other Americans returning to their European ancestral homes for the first time react? What about the experience of the many Jewish people from various parts of the world returning to Israel for the first time, particularly those from North Africa? To overlook this universal fact is to miss the sociological significance of the marginal man. To scrutinize the black Americans in Africa without examining comparable situations elsewhere does injustice to the relationships concerned. How does one account for the scientific literature concerning "marginal" people in the United States who move from rural areas into towns and cities?

Another writer who shares Isaacs' view in his study of the relationships between Africans and American blacks is Russell Howe (1961).[38] Howe discusses some issues concerning a successful black American agricultural expert, towards whom the African chief and his citizens manifested a disapproving attitude. The Africans are said to have laughed at the expert because he had installed in his house:

an electric generator and air-conditioning in his administra-
tive bungalow; he had bought up frozen food from the
capital and stored it in the freezer; he was touchy about
what he and especially about what his wife and children
ate. In other words, he had tried to make life as comfortable and healthy as the situation permitted in this land of
amoebic dysentery. All these things would have been forgiven if he had been English or French or white American.
But Robert Jones and his wife were Negro.[39]

Are highly educated black Africans, particularly those educated abroad, exempt from contempt by their own people, if
they also act like this American black? Certainly empirical.
data paint a very different picture. For example, Mr. Jones
seems to fall into the same social-class situation as any overseas educated African. He has high education and a good job,
and we assume he draws a fairly good salary for his services.
If we turn to Africans comparable to Mr. Jones in status and
examine how other Africans react to them, our picture of this
issue is quite different and clear.

Hodgkin and Schachter (1960) discuss the "radical opposition" directed to already established political figures by the
African overseas university-trained students.[40] Apter (1963)
gives a sensitive analysis of intellectual conflicts in Ghana
among the "seventh-form boys" and the university-trained;
he aptly summarizes the conflict as one between *petite* and
grande intelligentsia.[41] Bantom (1957:120) discusses attacks
by African laboring classes on westernized Africans who wore
ties during riot conditions.[42] Goldthorpe (1961:156) emphasizes that in time of stress, for example, during the Mau Mau
War and riot in Uganda, those Africans under attack were those
who were seen to be the "most" westernized Africans, e.g.,
Mindele ndobe (Southern Africa), *Wazungu weusi* (East Africa),
and *Been-to* (West Africa).[43] In black America, those who are
trying to be white are called "Uncle Toms" or "Oreos." Whatever the nation, common terms are used to describe characteristics and behaviors of individuals who behave in a Western
manner. They do not have to come from a different geographi-

cal area, but it is a black people's description of certain mannerisms and behavioral patterns perceived as foreign. It is not
the job, the money, or where one is educated; it is the attitudes
and behavioral patterns that result. Reference to the unedu-
cated masses of poor Africans as *Washenzis* (savages) or a black
American reference to other blacks as "niggers" would not carry
different significance if the speaker were a black American in
Africa or an African in Africa.

An important point made by Howe's discussion of Mr. Jones's
case is typical of the ambiguous situation that faces American
Negroes in Africa, as the State Department, the black university,
and the American business companies ". . . think that because
he is the Negro—'Afro-American,'—he will be more acceptable
to African people. In some cases, of course, Negroes are eager
to go to Africa out of curiosity and sympathy."[44]

Why shouldn't American blacks be acceptable in Africa because they are blacks? Does it necessarily matter that quality
has something to do with the way the job is done? Or are nonblacks just as susceptible to failure and disenchantment?

Howe goes on to warn the State Department, the universities,
and the American private companies that

> ". . . on the whole, the policy of using a large number of
> American Negroes in African jobs *is dangerous* for all con-
> cerned—the employer, the usually discontented or dis-
> enchanted Negroes, the natives and the United States."[45]
> [emphasis added]

However, Howe does not address himself to whether or not
whites who become "disenchanted and discontented" would
be less dangerous. Are the relationships of the white Americans
abroad with the natives always happy, and do they avoid dis-
content?

What has been suggested is that there has been a Eurocentric
view when it comes to studying the relationships between black
Americans and Africans. This view was aptly summed up by
Charles A. Valentine when he stated:

What these scholars accomplished by misapplying an in-
accurate and irrelevant theory of social classes to Black
people should be clear. They denied the existence of an
Afro-American culture heritage. They presented a most
distorted and degrading picture of Black communities.
Most fundamental, they totally misunderstood the past,
present, and future courses of developing White-Black
relations. These points, taken together, make up the core
of what we have called the mainstream approach. This
again demonstrates the great need for an approach which
stresses the primarily ethnic and racial dimensions of the
Afro-American situation and its problems, an emphasis
which is now being developed by Black Studies.[46]

The Eurocentric view of the study of black relations that
Valentine called the "mainstream" perspective maintains, as
has been shown, that black culture does not exist. Whatever
does exist is attributed to black communal "pathology" or the
slave South; the conclusion is that whatever exists is not worth
guarding or preserving.
    In our next chapter, we shall examine the second premise,
the "Afrocentric perspective." Unlike the Eurocentric view,
which denies the existence of distinctive black American
cultural creations, the "Afrocentric" perspective maintains that
they do exist. The fact that they do not fit within the larger
context of the American cultural mainstream, the Afrocentric
perspective argues, does not necessarily mean they are "pathological" but means rather that they originate within the continent of Africa.

Notes

1. Nathan Glazer and Daniel Patrick Moynihan, *Beyond the Melting
Pot* (Cambridge, Mass.: M.I.T. and Harvard University Press, 1963); E.
Franklin Frazier, *The Negro Family in the United States* (Chicago: The
University of Chicago Press, 1966).
    2. Gunnar Myrdal, *The American Dilemma: The Negro Problem and
Modern Democracy* (New York: Harper and Brothers, 1944).

3. Ibid., p. 11.

4. Carl N. Degler, "The Negro in America—Where Myrdal Went Wrong," in *New York Times Magazine*, December 7, 1969, pp. 155, 156.

5. Glazer and Moynihan, *Beyond the Melting Pot*, p. 53.

6. Ibid., p. xx.

7. Frazier, *The Negro Family*, p. 257.

8. Ibid., pp. 257, 265.

9. Ibid., p. 367.

10. Ibid., pp. 257, 265.

11. Ibid., p. 365.

12. Michael Harrington, *The Other America: Poverty in the United States* (New York: Macmillan, 1962).

13. Charles A. Valentine, *Culture and Poverty: Critique and Counter-Proposals* (Chicago: The University of Chicago Press, 1968), pp. 20, 22, 23.

14. Gerald McWorter, "The Ideology of Black Social Science," *The Black Scholar* (December 1969): 30.

15. Jackquelyne J. Jackson, "But Where Are the Men," *The Black Scholar* (December 1971): 36n.

16. Elliot Liebow, *Tally's Corner: A Study of Negro Streetcorner Men* (Boston: Little, Brown, 1960).

17. Herbert G. Gutman, *The Black Family in Slavery and Freedom 1750-1925* (New York: Pantheon Books, 1976), pp. vii-xx.

18. James M. Davis, Russel G. Hansen, and Duane R. Burnor, *IIE Survey of the African Student: His Achievements and His Problems* (New York: Institute of International Education, 1961).

19. Ibid., p. 27.

20. Ibid.

21. Ibid.

22. John Livingston, "The African Student in the United States," Howard University (New York: Schomburg Collection, New York Public Library N.Y.), 1968, pp. 6-7.

23. Raymond N. Logan, "The American Negro's View on Africa," *Présence Africaine* (New York: Schomburg Collection, New York Public Library, 1969), p. 226.

24. Ibid.

25. Ibid.

26. Ibid., pp. 226-227.

27. Joseph Veroff, "African Students in the United States," *Journal of Social Issues* (19 July 1963).

28. Ibid., p. 52.

29. U.S. Advisory Commission on International Educational and Cul-

tural Affairs, *Foreign Students in the United States: A National Survey*, Washington, D.C., 1966.

30. Ernest J. Wilson, "A Survey of Attitudes and Interests of Foreign Students at Howard University, 1965." As cited in Jane W. Jacqz, "African Students at U.S. Universities" (Report of a Conference on the Admission and Guidance of African Students held at Howard University, Washington, D.C., March 17-18, 1967), p. 60.

31. Richard T. Morris, *The Two-way Mirror: National Status in Foreign Student's Adjustment* (Minneapolis: University of Minnesota Press, 1960).

32. John Halston, "Black Africans and Black Americans on an American Campus: The African View" (Los Angeles: University of California, 1968), p. 35.

33. Ibid.

34. Ibid.

35. Harold R. Isaacs, "Back to Africa," *The New Yorker* (May 13, 1961).

36. Ibid., p. 105.

37. Ibid.

38. Russell Howe, "Strangers in Africa," *The Reporter* (June 22, 1961).

39. Ibid.

40. T. Hodgkin and Ruth Schachter, "French-Speaking West Africa in Transition," *International Conciliation* (May 1960).

41. David E. Apter, *Ghana in Transition* (New York: Atheneum, 1963).

42. Michael P. Bantom, *West African City* (London: Oxford University Press, 1957).

43. J. E. Goldthorpe, "Educated Africans: Some Conceptual and Terminological Problems in Aidan Southall." In *Social Change in Modern Africa* (London: Oxford University Press, 1961).

44. Howe, "Strangers in Africa," p. 35.

45. Ibid.

46. Charles A. Valentine, *Black Studies and Anthropology: Scholarly and Political Interests in Afro-American Culture* (Reading, Mass.: Addison-Wesley Modular Publications, 1972), Module No. 15, p. 9.

2.
Afrocentric View

Chapter 1 examined the Eurocentric view of black relationships that claims black Americans have no distinctive culture of their own and denies their distinctive cultural links to Africa. We now turn to our second set of perceptions, that there indeed exists a distinctive black American culture in the United States however small the degree of distinction, that the existing black American cultural manifestations have their roots within the larger continent of Africa, and that black Americans and Africans share an identification based on more than common ancestry.

To demonstrate the existence of black American and African identification, we shall first examine the literature that shows African cultural traits among black Americans. Second, we will consider various historical accounts that clearly show some black Americans' attempts to keep their African ties alive, including their constant struggles to return to the homeland, Africa. Third, we will look at two potent black movements—Pan Africanism and Garveyism—that articulated black peoples' ties with one another as well as a strong recognition of their ancestral roots.

Historical Accounts of Black American Identifications with Africa

Miles Mark Fisher (1969) has documented fully the painful struggles blacks went through in order to get back to Africa.[1]

He relates, for example, that many captured slaves jumped over-
board from slave ships, thinking that they could swim back to
their homelands and that even if they were not to make shore
through the vast ocean, at least their souls would. He cited an
incident that occurred in 1816 when Quakers in North Carolina bought numerous slaves in order to set them free. Among
those to be set free, most asked to "cross over" to Africa
rather than to go elsewhere. This desire to go back to Africa
ultimately gave rise to the establishment of Sierra Leone.
When a request was made in 1792 that three or four free
Negroes return to Africa to save their people, approximately
1200 blacks left both Canada and the United States to settle
in Sierra Leone.[2]

Shortly after blacks in the United States had been emancipated, they were viewed as a social problem. This complication
led Samuel Hopkins to suggest that freed Negroes should be
banished from America. Others were greatly criticized for free-
ing slaves as well as advocating expatriation from America.
Criticisms of banishment were made by those who held that
Negroes were making substantial contributions to the nation
and saw no good reasons for banishment. These criticisms did
not deter those who, for various reasons, wanted Negroes ejected
forever from "the land of the free." In December 1816, the
Society for Colonizing Free People of Color in the United States
was formed, led by a Presbyterian minister, Robert Finley, with
Thomas Jefferson's blessings.[3] The supporters of this venture
to expatriate black Americans from America were motivated
by two basic reasons. Some, like Finley, were motivated by
humanitarian reasons, and some were motivated by racial
prejudice.

Some blacks, after discovering that African repatriation was
based on racial grounds, refused to move from the United
States, even back to Africa. Most blacks who did not want to
be repatriated felt that they had built America by their labor.
It is not always true that those black Americans who refused
to go to Africa did so because they did not identify themselves
with Africa; rather, most of them felt they had contributed to
America, and hence they had the right to stay in the United

States like other ethnic groups. But white American racists
wanted America to become an exclusively white country;
others who held the black man's interests at heart joined because they believed "Negroes loved Africa."[4]

Louis Mehlinger (1916) has documented the black man's
struggle in America to return home to Africa.[5] Lynch (1966)[6]
further documented such attempts in the United States,
Canada, and the Caribbean Islands.[6] He pointed out that the
sentiment of Africans in the New World for their homeland
was alive, as manifested through different usages of the term
"Africa" in titles of many black organizations in America. Although many blacks could not return to Africa, their identification with Africa remained.

This strong passion among many Africans in the New World
to return home has existed for a long time. As Shepperson
pointed out:

> Some Negroes in America showed an interest in Africa be-
> fore the 1860's—usually in the face of the criticism of the
> Black abolitionists such as Frederick Douglass who con-
> sidered the African dream a dangerous diversion of ener-
> gies needed in the fight for emancipation and civil rights
> at home.[7]

Alexander Crummell has eloquently presented the black
Americans' quest for Africa in his correspondence material,
particularly those written by himself and Blyden.[8] After his
graduation from Queens College, Cambridge, he went to Liberia
in 1853 to "impress upon his countrymen their responsibility."[9]
While seeking to bring about reform in Liberia and to extend
its influence and jurisdiction over the inland peoples, Crummell
took a leading role in organizing schemes for exploring and
opening up the interior.[10] In his excitement, he brought back
encouraging information to America for the integrationists as
well as the emigrationists. The same trip took him to Nigeria,
where he managed to meet King Decemo of Lagos.

In a letter to his friend Garnet, Martin Delany had many
beautiful things to say about his impressions of Lagos. He also

managed to travel extensively in Nigeria for six weeks and at the end signed a treaty with the Obas and chiefs on December 27, 1895, to give as "a commissioner on behalf of the African in America, the right and privilege of settling in common with the Egba people, on any part of the territory belonging to Abeokuta, not otherwise occupied."[11] While in England, he again emphasized "our policy, must be . . . Africa for the African race and Black men to rule them."[12]

Delany's account of the receptions he received when he went to Africa in 1859 are overwhelming. He pointed out in his accounts: "In Monrovia I received a hero's welcome." Africans are said to have come "from all parts of the country to welcome me home." He stated that "the desire of African nationality has brought me to these shores."[13] He related how his immigration plan for black Americans to move to Africa was approved by those he called "the most eminent Liberians." All this excitement gave him "one of the most unforgettable and profound sensations of my life."[14] He was in Liberia to celebrate the Liberian Twelfth Annual Independence Day, which "came off with grand effect."[15] When Blyden and Crummell returned to Liberia in 1861, they were not only warmly received but appointed commissioners in order "to protect the cause of Liberia to the descendents of Africa and upon their sympathies, and the paramount advantages that would accrue to them, their children and their race by their return to the fatherland."[16]

Black American and African Identifications in the 1900s

A discussion of black American identifications with one another immediately recognizes William E. B. Du Bois, who provided exemplary leadership in the area of Afro-American and African relations.

Du Bois began his black cultural discussions in his book, *The Souls of Black Folk* (1903) and made major contributions in two areas.[17] He defined black American relationships to white Americans, first by analyzing the problematic nature of

the whole American economic structure and the resulting intergroup relationships, which he characterized as the black consciousness of culture differences and ethnic conflicts. According to Du Bois, if one were adequately to understand the nature
and extent of ethnic conflicts, a clear understanding of the
economic structure grounded within the historical framework
would be necessary. His second major contribution followed
from the first: he defined and portrayed major aspects of the
group life that expresses the distinctiveness of black American
life and culture.

In his attempt to understand the conditions of blacks in
America in relation to whites' background, he concluded that
many black people have what he called a "double-consciousness." He expressed this dilemma by saying that: "The Negro
is a sort of a seventh son, born within a veil, and gifted with
second sight in this American world." He added that America
"yields him no true self-consciousness, but only lets him see
himself through the revelation of the other world." He portrayed this other world as "a peculiar sensation, this double-
consciousness, this sense of always looking at oneself through
the eyes of others" and stated that "One ever feels his two-ness—
an American, a Negro: two souls, two thoughts, two unreconciled
strivings; two warring ideas in one dark body."[18]

Du Bois in his discussion of the plight of black people emphasized the "longing to attain self-conscious manhood, to
merge his double self into a better and truer self." Unlike others,
Du Bois does not say that black Americans were struggling to
assimilate but, rather, blacks "would not Africanize America"
nor would a black "bleach his Negro soul in a flood of white
Americanism." . . . For a black man, Du Bois stressed, "simply
wishes to make it possible for a man to be both a Negro and
an American, without being cursed and spit upon by his
fellows. . . ."[19]

In search for himself and his manhood, Du Bois had to examine his ancestral origins and about this he said:

> My African racial feeling was then purely a matter of my
> own later learning; my recoil from the assumptions of the

Whites; my experiences in the south at Fisk. But it was
nonetheless real and a large determinant of my life character. I feel myself African and an integral member of the
group of dark Americans who were called Negroes.[20]

His intellectual examination of "race" seemed to have left
him empty and puzzled him for a long time; finally he seemed
to have resolved this problem as he stated:

> Since then the concept of race has so changed and pre-
> sented so much of contradiction that as I face Africa I
> ask myself: What is it between us that constitutes a tie
> which I can feel better than I can explain? Africa is of
> course my fatherland. Yet neither my father nor my
> father's father ever saw Africa or cared over-much for it.
> My mother's folk were closer and yet their direct connec-
> tion, in culture and race, became tenuous: still, my tie to
> Africa is strong. On this vast continent were born and
> lived a large portion of my direct ancestors going back a
> thousand years or more.[21]

Through this long process of self-examination, he finally decided that identifications based upon color and ancestry alone
were not so important as those based upon the "social heritage" that bound people all over the world. Du Bois was very
much concerned with black people, although little in his own
background should have so disposed him. He was of upper-
class social background, a New Englander who had an excep-
tional academic record with little exposure to blacks. He claimed
descent from French Huguenots, so his concern for "social
heritage" rather than "color" is of interest here. He made it
very clear when he said:

> But one thing is sure and that is the fact that since the
> fifteenth century these ancestors of mine and their other
> descendants have had a common history; have suffered a
> disaster and have one long memory. The actual ties of
> heritage between individuals of this group vary with the

ancestors that they have in common and many others: Europeans and Semites, perhaps Mongolians, certainly Indians. But the physical bond is least and the badge of color relatively unimportant save as a badge; the real essence of this kinship is its social heritage of slavery; the discrimination and insult; and this heritage binds together not simply the children of Africa, but extends throughout yellow Asia and into the South Seas. It is this unity that draws me to Africa.[22]

One of Du Bois' major contributions was to point to the existence of a distinctive black American culture in America and to link it to African origins.

His study led him to a different light than had been shown before. He discovered African survivals in the New World embedded within black religion, magic, folklore, and music. The linkage did not stop here. He went on to put them within their rightful place. "The faith of the fathers," he wrote, "sprung from the African forests." To Du Bois, the traditional African medicine men became a major cultural medical link evolving in the New World, into black "bard, physician, judge, and priest, within the narrow limits allowed by the slave system" and for these, he felt, "rose the Negro preacher, and under him the first Afro-American institution, the Negro Church."[23]

During the early part of the twentieth century, the relationships between black Americans and Africans took on a different flavor. The Pan-African Movement was born in 1900. This association created a liaison between Africans in the New World and those on the African continent. Prior to this, the initiative of seeking unity among black Americans with Africans was predominantly a one-way venture, limited to efforts by black Americans in the New World. The Pan-African Movement defined the problem of black people not only locally, but internationally—wherever black people were to be found around the world. This new direction was important because it included those masses of people of color who were predominantly from what is now called the Third World.

As it has already been noted, Du Bois was struggling with his

identity and the identities of his people. In the end he concluded that the central issue was not basically that of ancestry
or color, but something beyond that—it was the lower social
status that comes as a result of economic conditions that seem
to govern peoples' lives. He mentioned that he shared these
problems with the American Indians, the Asians in Asia, and
those from the islands of the sea. Yet with none of these did
he share common ancestry or color. After he arrived at this
conclusion, he felt he had to wage war, an international war
against the injustices perpetrated by human beings on others.

Dr. W. E. B. Du Bois waged an international struggle against
suppression and oppression by Europeans of the masses of
people of color and particularly against Africans and their
descendants in the New World. He said, "The problem of the
Twentieth Century is the problem of the color line: the relation of the darker to the lighter races of men in Asia and Africa,
in America and the islands of the sea."[24]

He saw the problem of the masses tied to racial, political,
economic, and social forces:

> The history may be epitomized in one World Empire; the
> domination of White Europe over Black Africa and Yellow
> Asia, through political power built on the economic con-
> trol of labour, income and ideas. The echo of the industrial
> imperialism in America was expulsion of Black men from
> American democracy, this subjection to caste control and
> wage slavery.[25]

Identifications through the Pan-African Movement

The first Pan-African Conference was called in 1900 by
Henry Sylvester Williams, a barrister-at-law from Trinidad, who
had known some African students while in London. This Pan-
African Conference was the forerunner of the massively supported Pan-African Movement in Africa, the United States,
and the Caribbean islands of the 1960s.

The aim of the Pan-African Conference, as Williams put it, was to "bring into closer touch with each other people of African descent throughout the world."[26] This call for black unity was not without its difficulties. Black people were divided among themselves concerning the question of black American immigration to Africa. Those who were hopeful that American racial problems would somehow improve at home and blacks would be accepted as first-class citizens were epitomized by Booker T. Washington.

Booker T. Washington's published response to Williams' invitation to attend the first Pan-African Conference was met with indifference in America. Washington's and Du Bois' ideological feuds were well known in the black press. Washington had a large following among the grass-roots blacks, whereas Du Bois, through his publication *Crisis*, reached few middle-class readers. In the end, Washington wrote a letter, published in several Afro-American newspapers, in which he told of the work of Williams and Mason, as well as the plans for the Pan-African Conference. Washington, in a letter to Williams dated July 25, 1899, said,

> I beg and advise as many of our people as can possibly do so, to attend this conference. In my opinion, it is going to be one of the most effective and far reaching gatherings that has ever been held in connection with the development of the race.[27]

The letter appeared in the *Indianapolis Freeman*, a black weekly, on August 12, 1899. In spite of his endorsement, Washington declined to attend the conference personally, pointing out that he had other important business in the southern United States.

The Pan-African Conference became an intriguing issue in the press. Adolf Crabowski, in an article, "Tri-Continental Trilogy," that appeared in *Time of War*, made the following comment, which was characteristic of the fervent flavor of black American concern with Africa:

The American Negroes support the idea and give themselves up to it. Here, too, there is a strange reversal of things: To banish the Black peril to Africa, the United States, in the twenties of the last century, founded the Negro Republic of Liberia. Unneeded Blacks were to be transported to harmless Africa. Africa, however, has begun to move and reaches ever enticingly to America. The American Negro, aroused by Pan-African perspectives, furnished the home continent with their strengths; their spirits; their money.

The Pan-African Movement is supported by American Negroes who represent a not inconsiderable part of the population of the United States and whose purchasing power is a force more and more to be reckoned with.[28]

Indifference notwithstanding, the First Pan-African Conference convened in London at Westminster Hall on July 23-25, 1900. This initial conference was significant for among the delegates eleven were from America, four from Africa, and thirteen from the Caribbean islands. These black people had come together for a common purpose, having been separated by the cruel institution of slavery several centuries earlier. At this conference, the delegates adopted and sent out a memorandum that was presented to the British government by the Lord Bishop of London, Dr. Greighton. The memorandum protested against "acts of injustices directed against Her Majesty's subjects in South Africa and other parts of her dominions." A subsequent reply from the British government stating "Her Majesty's Government will not overlook the interests and welfare of the native races" was sent to Williams, who was then the Pan-African secretary general.

In his address to the conference, Du Bois emphasized the role played by the worldwide economic structures in suppressing and oppressing peoples of color, particularly in Africa. He made the remark that people of Africa should not be "sacrificed to the greed of gold, their liberties taken away." He felt that the British empire should give "the rights of responsible government to the black colonies of Africa and the West Indies" and also that Afro-Americans should be granted "the right of franchise, security of person and property. . . ."[29]

His concern for the masses of oppressed peoples led him to appeal for the following:

> Let the Nations of the world respect the integrity and independence of the free Negro States of Abyssinia, Liberia, Haiti and let the inhabitants of these States, the independent tribes of Africa, the Negroes of the West Indies and America, and the black subjects of all nations take courage, strive ceaselessly, and fight bravely, that they may prove to the world their incontestable right to be counted among the great brotherhood of mankind.[30]

During the interim period between the First Pan-African Conference in 1900 and the First Congress on February 19-21, 1919, there emerged other efforts in the United States to unite black people in their struggle to return to their homeland. One such effort was that of the influential movement started by Marcus Garvey, spanning from 1918 to 1928. Garvey rose to take up the task of "African redemption" through his powerful organizations, the Universal Negro Improvement Association and the African Communities League, and the newspaper, the *Negro World.* He appealed to the masses because he "projected various means and enterprises which appealed to and afforded expression of his basic human desire."[31]

Garvey had travelled widely in the southern United States, Central America, and England. Earlier, during his stay in England from 1912 to 1914, he met and worked with an Egyptian scholar and editor of the *African Times and Orient Review*, Dr. Ali Duse Mohamed, and from this strong African nationalist Garvey got most of his ideas about Africa and Africans, as well as the slogan "Africa for the Africans." This slogan had already appeared in America in a booklet, *Africa for the African*, written twenty years before by Joseph Booth, a British missionary who had worked both in Natal, South Africa, and in Malawi, then "Nyasaland." The booklet was published in Baltimore, Maryland, in 1897.

Booth met John Chilembwe and later helped Chilembwe travel to the United States to study in Lynchburg, Virginia.[32] Chilembwe was influenced by some prominent black American nationalists, and he went back to Africa, taking with him his nationalistic ideas. He protested the use of Nyasaland soldiers who were sent to fight against the Ashantis of West Africa. Later he opposed the recruitment of Africans to fight in World War I, in which he was to lose his own life.[33]

When Marcus Garvey came to the United States to confer with Booker T. Washington, he found blacks disorganized, impoverished, and chaotic. He immediately set out to bring about unity among his people: he talked of the science of economics and its application to their lives; he lectured about the history, culture, religion, customs, and traditions of their ancestral land, Africa. He asked, ". . . where is the black man's government? Where is his president, his country, and his ambassadors, his army, his navy, and his men of big affairs? I could not find them."[34]

Garvey was branded a racist and lumped together with other enemies of the black people such as the Ku Klux Klan and the Anglo-Saxon Club. It is rather difficult, however, to classify Garvey as a racist. It is quite evident that Garvey was seeking racial pride and freedom for the oppressed masses. He felt that people should have the right to determine their own destinies:

> Each race should be proud and stick to its own and the best of what they are should be shown. This is no shallow song of hate to sing, but over Blacks there should be no White Kings.

> Every man on his own foothold should stand, claiming a nation and a fatherland! White, Yellow, and Black should make their own laws, and force no one-sided justice with flaws.[35]

In his proclamation of black pride he said, "Be as proud of your race today as our fathers were in the days of yore. We

have a beautiful history, and we shall create another in the future that will astonish the world."[36] These are not racist ideas,
but ideas of justice. When Garveyism was at its peak, it became
difficult for the Pan-African Conference to convene. The black
community had been divided into two equally strong factions,
one led by Du Bois and his Pan-Africanist Movement, with predominantly black, middle-class intellectual followers, and the
other led by Garvey, comprised primarily of the black masses
who were striving to exist from day to day in America. The
ideological as well as the tactical differences between these two
black leaders have been described by Colin Legum as follows:

> Du Bois and Garvey were great rivals. Du Bois, a Negro
> of mixed blood, tiresomely proud of his own Dutch and
> French ancestors, and especially of the suggestion of
> Huguenot nobility; Garvey, a black Jamaican.
>
> Du Bois, a vain, prickly, egocentric intellectual, deliberate-
> ly avoiding mass appeals; Garvey, a rodomontade rabble-
> rouser, who, at the height of his career, could with some
> justification claim the support of millions of Negroes and
> command vast sums of their money.
>
> Garvey mocked Du Bois for his light color, and refused
> to cooperate with light-skinned Negroes whom he de-
> nounced as "hybrids." Du Bois dismissed Garvey as a
> "little, fat, black man; ugly but intelligent eyes and a big
> head!" Although the ideas that divided them are no longer
> deeply relevant, both men are prototypes of African
> political leaders; and their attitudes are deeply revealing.[37]

The first Pan-African Congress met soon after the end of
World War I, February 19-20, 1919, in Paris. Here Du Bois met
Blaise Diagne, the African deputy from Senegal and commis-
sioner-general for the recruitment of African troops. At this
conference were nine African delegates, sixteen from the United
States, and twenty-one from the West Indies. Du Bois pointed
out, however, that most of these delegates did not come to
France to attend the conference but just happened to have been

in Paris for different reasons at the time, in particular to attempt
to influence the Versailles Peace Conference. It seems that
these people were black intellectuals or black community leaders
who could afford to pay their own way to Paris.

The Second Pan-African Conference met at three different
places: in London, August 28-29, 1921; in Brussels, August 31-
September 2, 1921; and in Paris, September 4, 1921. This conference had a large number of African representatives, forty-one
in all, with twenty-four Afro-Americans and seven representatives
from the Caribbean islands. The conference adopted resolutions
criticizing the Belgian regime in the Congo, and they affirmed
that of ". . . all the various criteria of which masses of men in
the past have been prejudged, that of the color of the skin
and the texture of the hair is surely the most adventitious and
idiotic." This conference made eight demands for Africans.
Six of these were:

1. A voice in their own government
2. Native rights to the land and its natural resources.
3. Modern education for all children.
4. The development of Africa for the Africans and not
   merely for the profit of Europeans.
5. The reorganization of commerce and industry so as to
   make the main object of capital and labor the welfare
   of the many rather than the enriching of the few.
6. The treatment of civilized men as civilized despite differences of birth, race or color.[38]

Du Bois tried to organize the Fourth Pan-African Conference
in 1925, but it failed for many different reasons. One reason
Du Bois cited was sabotage by those powers who saw the movement as detrimental to their political and economic interests.
For example, the French over-priced their sea liners that were
to be chartered for the conference. After the initial setback,
the Fourth Conference was convened in 1927. The Fourth Conference was spearheaded by American Negro women and met
in New York, instead of on one of the Caribbean Islands as
originally planned by Du Bois. The American Negro Women's
Congress published a pamphlet giving particulars about itself:[39]

1. "Pan" gives it the significance "all African."
2. Pan-African is those parts of the world where the percentage of populations of African descent is sufficiently large to cause a so-called "color" problem.
3. What is Pan-African Congress? A Pan-African Congress is a meeting of persons of Negro descent belonging to those widely scattered groups and citizens of different countries, for the purpose of fuller and more perfect acquaintance and understanding, as well as for the exposition and suppression of the many problems of race and social uplift which today confront these groups.
4. The question of the status of the Negro in modern society is no longer a domestic problem of the United States, or a parochial problem of Jamaica, or a colonial policy problem. It is rather a great worldwide problem to be viewed and considered as a whole, and Congress particularly desires that the relations of the black and white race in various countries be considered to the end that greater harmony may ensue.
5. Is Pan-African Congress a migratory, "back-to-Africa" movement? No. The Pan-African Congress is not and never has been interested in a scheme of immigration to Africa or elsewhere. It believes in the equality of men and races everywhere, but seeks to realize this through education, opportunity and periodic conferences.
6. Is Pan-African Conference a political organization? No. The Pan-African Congress has no political affiliations in any community. It aims to be an open forum of opinion and it has no connections expressed or implied, with other organizations beyond its general objects.[40]

Among the two hundred and eight delegates, only four African countries were represented (Sierra Leone, Liberia, Nigeria, and the Gold Coast). The Congress received wide publicity and mixed feelings in the press. *The New York Amsterdam News* reported:

The proceedings of the later Pan-African Congress should be closely followed by all students of racial phenomena.

With delegates from all countries having an African population they reveal the problems and needs of the Negro
the world over are substantially the same.[41]

The Congress was reported to have registered major concern
for blacks in Africa and all over the world:

> . . . Whenever it is proven that African natives are not re-
> ceiving just treatment at the hands of any state or that
> any state deliberately excludes its civilized citizens or sub-
> jects of Negro descent, it shall be the duty of the League
> of Nations to bring the matter to the attention of the
> civilized world.[42]

During the same meeting, the Gold Coast delegation, led by
Chief Nana Amoah III, asked that "American Negroes send scientific men to Africa to assist the Africans in developing their
own resources and secure some measure of relief from European domination."[43] *The Chicago Bee* reported that William
Pickens, field secretary of the National Association for the
Advancement of Colored People (NAACP), had said:

> In spite of the powerful tradition of the myth of race we
> wish to say that a likeness in economic condition is a far
> sounder basis for cooperation among men than in a simi-
> larity of skin color or nose shape. . . .

> The Pan-African Congress, a biennial Conference of all the
> descendants of Africa throughout the world, was con-
> ceived by Dr. Du Bois. . . . It recognizes the fact that in a
> world largely dominated by group-conscious white men
> there are color problems for the colored people of the
> world, and especially for the descendants of Africa. . . .
> Economic exploitation knows neither race nor color. It
> will attack that group which is most helpless, most open
> to exploitation. The Negroes of Africa were not enslaved
> because they were Negroes, but because they offered the
> greatest return for the small amount of outlay and effort
> to the slave hunter. Capitalist exploiters are a natural class

not to be distinguished by race, color, language or ancient history.[44]

Here the idea of a purely racial identity is denied; the Pan-African saw the problem as being economically motivated, a class struggle that concerns not only the black peoples of the world but all people who are oppressed. The evil was not only whites against blacks but exploiters against the exploited.

The next Pan-African Congress did not meet until October 12-21, 1945, in the Chorlton Hall at Manchester, England.[45] George Padmore was the Secretary of the Pan-African Foundation. The conference elected joint political secretaries, George Padmore and Kwame Nkrumah, while Jomo Kenyatta was elected Assistant Secretary and Dr. Du Bois designated as Chairman of the Platform Committee and unanimously elected International President of the Pan-African Congress. He subsequently took the role of the elder statesman, the "Grand Old Man of Pan-Africanism," the "*Mzee.*" This Congress, more than any other, was one of the most significant in the history of the Pan-African Movement. Among the delegates were Africans who were later to lead their own countries to independence from colonial domination and further the aspirations of the Pan-African Congress. In 1957, when Ghana became the first African (black) nation to gain its independence from Britain, among those special guests invited by Kwame Nkrumah and his government were some dignitaries from the old vanguard of the Pan-African Movement from the United States, the Caribbean Islands, and Africa. They witnessed the moment when the Union Jack was lowered for the last time on Ghanian soil and in its place was raised the new Ghanian flag with the original colors of the Pan-African Movement, colors formerly intended for Garvey's new independent First African Republic.

Jomo Kenyatta of Kenya, who later was to lead his country to independence in 1963, also played a major role at this important congress. Hastings Kamuzu Banda of Malawi, Ja-Ja Wachuku, and O. Awolowo of Nigeria were also there, as were Peter Abrahams, a distinguished South African literary figure, and J. C. deGraft, a distinguished Ghanian historian.

The delegates stated that they:

Affirm the right of all Colonial Peoples to control their
own destiny. All colonies must be free from foreign
imperialists' control, whether political or economic. . . .
We say to the people of the colonies that they must fight
for those ends by all means at their disposal.[46]

The Manchester Pan-African Congress marked a turning point.
The Congress took on a more militant stand against white oppres
sion. Perhaps it was not coincidental that various liberation
movements in the African colonies were given impetus while
the cultural Pan-African revolutions were being carried forward
in America and in Europe. The journal *Présence Africaine*, with
Alioune Diop as its editor, was begun in Paris in 1947, followed
by the development of the Society of African Culture in Paris
and the Associated American Society of African Culture
(AMSAC) in the United States.

With the newly emerging African States, the First Conference of African States was held in Accra, April 12-22, 1958.
This was closely followed by several All Peoples Conferences
at Accra, 1958; Tunis, 1960; Cairo, 1961; Monrovia, 1961; and
the Summit Conference of May 22-25, 1963, followed by
another in Cairo in 1964.

Those black leaders present at the historical meeting in
Manchester had the following responses to the republication
in 1963 of the *History of the Pan-American Congress*. Nnamdi
Azikiwe, then the President of Nigeria, in his goodwill message,
said the 1945 Congress "marked the turning point in Pan-
Africanism from a passive to an active state." Du Bois remarked: "It carries messages which must not die, but should
be passed on to aid mankind and to inspire the darker races
of man to see themselves of one blood with all human beings.
. . . For that was a decisive year in determining the freedom of
Africa." President Mzee Jomo Kenyatta of Kenya reflected:
"The Congress was a landmark in the history of the African
people's struggle for unity and freedom." Mrs. George Padmore
said: "Its resolutions and resulting programmes inspired the
leaders who participated in its deliberations to carry forward
their endeavors in their native territories."[47]

A brief assessment of both the Garvey and Du Bois movements seems to indicate that, at least, the potent back-to-Africa movement that had stirred the black masses' spirits finally failed. Why did it fail after such formidable beginnings? The answer has been adequately provided by C. Eric Lincoln, who cited four major reasons. First, it failed because Garvey's plans for massive migration were ill-conceived and not effectively executed. Second, the monumental task far exceeded Garvey's and his officers' abilities. Third, history was against him because time was not yet ripe for such a venture. Fourth, he was fighting against strong colonial powers in Africa, the American government, the black middle class, and their white allies, who felt, for various reasons, threatened by Garvey's ventures to export masses of black people from the United States to Africa.[48]

Though Garvey's Back-to-Africa Movement was considered a failure, it nonetheless was given credit for having contributed the seeds of black pride: pride in one's skin color, in one's race, and in black peoples' African origin. Du Bois' Pan-African Movement helped to link up black intellectuals from America, the Caribbean islands, and Africa and fought to free people of color from colonialism. The Pan-African Movement with Du Bois as its leader was going on simultaneously with the Back-to-Africa Movement with Garvey as its leader. As it has been noted, these two black movements appealed to different black audiences. That is, Garvey appealed to predominantly black lower-class masses in America who did not seem hopeful that things were going to change for the better. To these masses, their last hope was to go back home to Africa and build a nation of their own with native Africans.

The second audience, the Pan-Africanists, were predominantly of the black middle class or the "talented tenth," as the Negro intellectuals called themselves. This group comprised intellectuals who had been relatively successful in America and as a result were much more hopeful that America as a nation would eventually change to include them in the ranks of humanity. Racial or cultural identifications with Africa and Africans were manifested least among this group. As Lincoln points out, the middle-class intellectuals "were not identifying with blackness" but rather "they were simply willing to discuss it in a detached, disinterested way. Only since the emergence of self-governing African states have the Negro intellectuals felt secure enough to risk some degree of identification."[49]

Let not the attitudes of black middle-class peoples be misunderstood here, that their lack of identification with blackness or Africa and Africans was final. Rather, they took another step—they rejected whiteness in America as well, in a "rejection of the traditional order of values which, because they cannot be attained with reasonable effort, are productive of increasing anxiety and frustration."[50]

This group joined the rest of the black people as expressed in

> . . . a rejection of integration (sometimes, as an insistence on separation). It does not necessarily imply a hatred for the White man, but it does imply a negation of the symbols of his culture, his power and his status. The tendency is, as it was expressed by a Harlem minister, to "let the White man go his way—but get him out of *my* way—and fast." But then, it is easy to hate what you negate. The Negro has a long and painful experience of that fact.[51]

Kwame Nkrumah, also speaking in this vein, said:

> When I speak of Africa for Africans, this should be interpreted in the light of my emphatic declaration that I do not believe in racialism and colonialism. The concept of "Africa for Africans" does not mean that other races are excluded from it. No. It only means that Africans, who naturally are the majority in Africa, shall and must govern themselves in their own countries. The fight is for the future of humanity, and it is a most important fight.[52]

These were conscious political and intellectual efforts, but at the same time there were behaviors, customs, and attitudes expressed within the masses of blacks (many lower-class) that indicated the influence of the African past.

Identification through Cultural Roots

Herskovits contributed in his works a great deal to better understanding of Afro-American ties to Africa in three major areas. He started by debunking myths and stereotypes about Africans and their descendants in the New World.[53] He warned scholars interested in the area by stating: ". . . the first step, then, is to debunk some of the myths of the Great White Society . . . [including the belief] that it is a kind society which is aiming at approaching perfection in its institutional systems, including its educational system."[54]

He set out to trace some Afro-Americans' distinctive social-cultural creations to their rightful origin—the continent of Africa. He studied black Americans' lives and discovered that they did possess sociocultural patterns of their own. He did not stop here but went further by boldly asserting that these distinctive black American cultural "survivals" have also percolated into the larger American culture.[55] His bold assertions caused a storm from all quarters. (This debate will be discussed later.) Herskovits' work helped foster a better approach to the understanding and study of Afro-Americans.[56] As a result of moving back in attempts to explain black American "double-consciousness," Herskovits, a student of Franz Boas, a noted critic of Darwinism and genetic theories, finally became the only Euro-American scholar of his time to examine black American culture from a black peoples' perspective by asserting that meaningful cultural differences still exist between black and white Americans in the United States.

Herskovits was greatly influenced in his thinking by Boas, opposing racism by countering biological and genetic explanations of differences among races and clearly pointing out that culture is learned rather than inherited, as had been assumed before. Herskovits' work provided the impetus for various social scientists to look into the problem more seriously, and most embarked upon cross-cultural research. Most researchers have discovered the existence of links from the Old World to the New, as Herskovits did.

In the field of religion, for example, Erika Bourguignon

(1967, 1970a, and 1970b) found cultural links originating from faith and rituals practiced among blacks in the New World that were the same as those practiced in Africa.[57]

In the field of folk arts, John Szwed (1970b) discovered links between Afro-American sacred and secular music and that found in Africa.[58] The use of various musical instruments, as well as events used for different reasons in Latin America, were found by Norman Whitten (1970) to be closely related to their use in Africa.[59] Alan Lomax (1970) has indicated that, through the use of the "cantometrics" technique, Afro-American music is closely related to "typical African song styles" and reflects little or no Western influence.[60] In the area of folk-tales, Daniel Crowley (1970) indicated that Afro-American folk-tales, especially those found throughout the Caribbean, are the same as those found in West Africa.[61]

These findings all point to the existence of a distinctive black American culture in the United States, as well as the fact that its cultural creations have their roots in Africa.

We shall now turn to some illustrations from black American history showing that black Americans in America never really forgot their original home, Africa. This does not mean, of course, that all black Americans were eagerly yearning to return to Africa; rather, this is an attempt to describe from history those who did. History also indicates that some black Americans, particularly the middle and upper classes, the intellectuals and the economically "better-off," indeed, did not want to identify themselves with Africa, let alone actually attempt to cross over to Africa. Our major concern here is to seek out examples from history and show that some black Americans have been trying to return to Africa since they were forcefully torn away from home. They have identified with Africa and Africans throughout history. There is ample evidence to show that though the Africans in the New World were forcefully held in bondage in a foreign and hostile land, their desire to return to Africa was always existent. It was a black consciousness, as manifested through American blacks' experiences in America. This is demonstrated predominantly in black American peoples in their arts as well as in their private lives.

Richard Wright, following the same cultural theme, described
". . . a culture of the Negro which has been addressed to him
and him alone, a culture which has, for good or ill, helped
clarify his consciousness and create emotional attitudes which
are conducive to action."[62] Wright attributed this black cultural
distinctiveness to first the Negro church and second to the
fluid folklore of the Negro people. He gave a solution to the
problem of "double consciousness" by suggesting that "if we
choose to stand on the side of social progress, then our artistic
expression must shape the folk-national aspirations of our
people."[63]

Another aspect of this black American consciousness was
the major role the Negro church played in keeping in close
touch with Africa, as documented by Shepperson.[64] It is safe
to say that among all the black institutions that had had long
and continuous influence in Africa, the Negro church was the
most influential. The church was a pioneer in sponsoring
African students who would study in the United States for a
time before returning to their own countries. The black church's
donations for missionary work and building schools, churches,
and hospitals are well-known.

The black American consciousness that Du Bois called a
"double consciousness" was later echoed by Ralph Ellison, who
summed it up as follows:

> In brief, there is an American Negro idiom, a style and way
> of life, but none of this is separate from the conditions
> of America's society nor from its general modes of cul-
> ture. . . . If a general American value influences us, we in
> turn influence them . . . and this despite the fact that
> nothing which Black Americans have won as a people has
> been won without a struggle.[65]

Eldridge Cleaver, responding to the concept of black "double-
consciousness," pointed out that "from the beginning, America
has been a schizophrenic nation."[66] Vincent Harding, a black
historian, says: "We have been forced to be both black and
white in America . . . are dangerous because we suggest to the

society that we are simply the vanguard of all those who must one day awake from the dream of America."[67]

The fact that black Americans throughout the centuries have had to be Americans as well as blacks at the same time, striving to be human beings as well as Americans, has led others to conclude that they have no past. But those with an Afrocentric view recognize the African traits of black people that have survived through history.

For example, Smith has pointed out that blacks in America, like Africans, are an oral people: "Black-Americans are essentially an oral people much like their African ancestors who found the expressive word to be the basis of society."[68] LeRoi Jones recognized black Americans' African musical survivals when he pointed out that:

> The most apparent survival of African music in Afro-
> American music are its rhythms: not only the seeming
> emphasis in the African music or rhythmic, rather than
> melodic or harmonic, qualities, but also the use of
> polyphonic, or contrapuntal, rhythmic effects. Because
> of this seeming neglect of harmony and melody,
> Westerners thought the music "primitive." It did not occur
> to them that Africans might have looked askance at a
> music as vapid rhythmically as the west's.[69]

What all these do is point out that black Americans have a past, a history, and a distinctive culture of their own. Those who deny them this past have often based their arguments on those few black American individuals who were middle class and often intellectuals and marginal people. Harold Cruse characterized the black middle class during the Harlem Renaissance in the 1920s as follows:

> . . . discussing of James Weldon Johnson's weak neutrality
> on the question of Negro vs. White creative competition,
> and his reluctance to come to critical grips with such
> obvious failures as the Harlem Renaissance, was the *class
> factor* in the Negro Movement of the 1920's; for the

Negro bourgeois-middle class stratum did not support the Harlem Renaissance Movement morally, aesthetically, or financially. The Negro middle-class being politically, socially, and economically marginal, was both unwilling and unable to play any commanding role in the politics and economics of culture and art, as either patrons or entrepreneurs.[70]

The example of a very few people, by Du Bois' estimate, the "talented tenth," should not be taken to indicate that all or most black Americans did not identify themselves with Africa.

Black American and African Identifications Today

We should turn next to recent years to see where some of these older strands of black American and African identifications are now, including the Pan-African Movement that Du Bois and others toiled so hard to start and maintain.

The Pan-African Movement in the 1970s was "quickly becoming a wide-spread, mass-based movement," *The Black Bulletin* announced.[71] For example, Owusa travelled to Africa and made contacts with the Revolutionary Forces of Mozambique Liberation Front. After this experience he came back to the United States and helped organize the largest demonstration of African solidarity since Marcus Garvey.

There was progress also on the cultural front. The African Heritage Studies Association, made up of scholars of African descent, was formed in 1969; its major aims were "the preservation, interpretation, and academic presentation of the history and cultural heritage of African peoples on ancestral soil of Africa and in the African diaspora." They also sought "the reconstruction of African history and cultural studies along Afrocentric lines, while effecting an intellectual union among Black scholars the world over."[72]

Two major questions that remain to be asked are: Where does the Pan-African Movement stand now? Are black Africans

and Americans identifying with each other? One of the best
answers is given in *The Black Bulletin: A Black Nationalist
Newsletter*, which warns that "the time is at hand when the
Black man must pause, and take serious note of the rapid current of world events." The struggle is not confined to local
spheres of influence; it has gone further than that.

> Life for people of African stock has been, for the past
> three centuries, a relentless struggle for survival. Not so
> much against the forces of nature, nay! Nature has blessed
> the African race with the richest of all continents, and
> the finest of all climates, and it has equipped the Black
> man with the greatest and most rugged physique among
> men, together with a woman whose wholesome beauty,
> sparkling eyes, rhythmic gait, warm tender smile, cheer-
> ful and affectionate disposition, cannot be excelled or
> rivalled by any other female.
>
> The Black man's menace has been, and still is, the white
> man's diabolical and determined plan to commit genocide!
> Even as they exterminated the American Indians, so too,
> every plan, every scheme, points to their murderous intent
> to liquidate the African people.[73]

Here too, the nationalists know who they are: "people of
African stock." Also, they have identified clearly the black
man's menace, "the white man." After this clear statement,
then what? What steps, if any, are black people taking to ensure
their ties?

It took almost thirty years for black people to organize and
call for the Sixth Pan-African Conference. It took place on
June 19-27, 1974, in Dar-es-Salaam, Tanzania. President of
Tanzania Mwalimu Julius Nyerere played key roles both as
the conference president and as host.

In 1974, unlike the Fifth Pan-African Conference in 1945,
most African and Caribbean governments were politically free
and independent. The delegates to the conference represented
governments, liberation movements, black organizations, and
interested individuals. In all, over 500 attended. As a participant

in the 1945 Conference, T. Ras Makonnen, originally from Guyana and living in Kenya, provided a special link between the old guard of Pan-Africanists and the new.

No sooner had the participants been seated than conflicting expectations and opinions began to appear. For example, black Americans had hoped that independent African nations would be able to welcome home blacks from the Diaspora just as Israel had done for the Jews, but they were disappointed when this did not occur. Even President Nyerere, who extended a welcome home, emphasized that his welcome was for black Americans who were "skilled workers and specially trained technologists." Most black Americans viewed Nyerere's announcement, however, as an important step in the right direction, toward total acceptance and admission of any blacks who might wish to move to Africa to live.[74]

Black Africans were also baffled by black Americans' "lack of strategic organization and effective leadership." This problem was aptly pointed out by Lucy Lammeck, a member of the Tanzanian delegation when she told a group of American women at a reception, "You people are disorganized." She added, "I heard them at a meeting. I thought they were going to kill each other the way they were at each other's throats."[75]

A major problem that seemed to plague the Sixth Congress as a whole related to its failure to establish any permanent machinery to implement over fifty Congress resolutions that emanated from three different committees dealing with political, economic, cultural, scientific, and technological matters. Most of the work was left for completion to Nyerere as president of the congress. He was asked to find ways to implement the terms of the resolutions. Nyerere said he "would ask the OAU to embrace the goals of the Congress and accept responsibility for keeping alive Pan-African connections, perhaps by establishing a special secretariat."[76]

Despite problems that plagued the Sixth Pan-African Congress, President Nyerere managed to take a bold step, attempting to keep alive conference ties. He told a group of scientists and technologists from Howard University that he was ready to commit Tanzania to the establishment of a Pan-African institute for scientific research. Reaffirming his strong Pan-African connections, he said, "I'm not going to wait until Africa makes up its mind to make up my mind to develop your ideas in Dar-es-Salaam."[77]

Although there were differences of opinions and real disappointments, most blacks agreed that the Sixth Pan-African Congress was a major welcome point concerning relations among black Africans and blacks from the Diaspora. Alma Robinson characterized the conference as follows:

> Spirits ran high because inspite of everything, everyone knew that it was a great event, this crossing of minds from a diverse number of directions for a common focal point. At the people-to-people level, the Congress was a fertile ground that may bear fruit for years to come.[78]

Black peoples' ties continued beyond the Pan-African conference; indeed significant relationships led to a higher plane of involvement and activism. One classic example is the work of a black organization, known as Transafrica. In a recent interview conducted by Anthony J. Hughes, Editor of *Africa Report*, Randall Robinson, Executive Director of Transafrica gave clues about where Pan-Africanism stands now.[79]

Transafrica was initiated and incorporated in 1977. One of its aims, among others, is to give black Americans opportunities "to be involved in the affairs of African people as those affairs are touched upon by U.S. policy." Transafrica draws people from across the nation and from "practically every professional discipline: labor, church, politics, and business." In 1980, the organization had about 10,000 members and hopes to raise its membership to 100,000 within two years by concentrating drives "in congressional districts where black people are found in great numbers so that we will have the leverage that we will need to have to impact on the Congress."[80] A newsletter is used to share up-to-date information of concern and interest to constituents on issues "that are before the Congress and the administration." The organization does "directly engage the administration here in meetings with the Secre-

tary of State, with the President, and members of Congress."
Likewise, the membership is urged through letters, telegrams,
and phone calls to convey their views to their representatives
in Congress and to the administration on issues which Transafrica has identified as issues of special concern.[81]

According to Robinson, his organization "fully intended to
be a mass organization. It is clear that we are not going to be
able to be effective unless we get rank-and-file black Americans
involved in the foreign policy process."[82]

When Robinson was asked whether or not individuals and
groups should be involved because of shared ideals rather than
involvements based specifically on the ties of black Americans
and Africans, he had this to say:

> I am not sure that your notion and mine are mutually ex-
> clusive ideas. It would be foolish of me to say that we
> don't welcome a collaborative kind of effort. We work
> shoulder to shoulder with the Washington office on
> Africa and with the American Committee on Africa be-
> cause as we organize our community, others organize
> their various constituencies. Going forward is much easier
> to do when we do it this way. It's much easier for us to
> organize our community. We have things to say to it that
> don't apply to the other communities. Blacks have an
> ancestral involvement and link with Africa that the other
> communities don't have and in that sense it is emotionally
> more important to us, perhaps even pragmatically. We
> see ourselves, in the larger sense, serving the broader
> interest of the country, of Africa, and the world. In as
> much as we are trying to build a bridge between ourselves
> and Africa, perhaps that bridge can also be useful to the
> United States as it learns how to respond more sensitively
> to the developing nations of Africa and, hopefully, to the
> developing world. I don't think that your problem has
> necessarily to be a problem. Because one appreciates
> ethnic homogeneity, it doesn't mean that precludes the
> involvement of others.[83]

Robinson spoke to the question whether or not black Americans as "underdogs" in the United States should focus their energies towards their own immediate domestic problems here at home rather than on issues of foreign policy:

> . . . Black Americans have been involved since the end of the Civil War, pushing first for the recognition of Liberia and Haiti, and have been involved since, so it's not really a new notion at all. One has to appreciate on another plane that we really can't afford to be parochial about this thing. The world is, in the final analysis, one place. I would say to those who think they can solve the problem in their cities without turning an eye to the problems of the nation or the problems of other nations, that's absolute poppycock, foolishness. What happens here affects people in other parts of the world. We live in a world community. While we concern ourselves with problems that seem more domestic than international, it doesn't mean that we can afford to ignore the rest of the world, at the same time. Human beings have to survive on this planet together, in a world that more equitably distributes the resources, and we have got to be a part of that. More specifically, as black Americans—to the extent that we have perceived ourselves as a tiny defenseless minority among a hostile and indifferent majority—we haven't had much leverage at all. But to the extent that we see ourselves as an integral part of an Africa on which the United States and the other Western powers are growing more dependent, then that gives us some leverage so that we can assist Africa in developing its own resources. By so doing we perhaps help to bring about some parity in the world. And that's to the advantage of black Americans as well. To the extent that it humanizes and sensitizes the United States and the other Western powers, I think it is to the overall advantage of the United States. The bottom line is that we just can't afford to see ourselves as citizens of Gary but not of Indiana, and again of the United States but not of the world—it's absolute foolishness.[84]

Transafrica works in the spirit of leaders like Du Bois to perceive domestic problems in terms of their worldwide implications. Although, it seems that Transafrica is concerned with black American and African problems and issues, nevertheless, it takes into account outside forces that seem to have impact on these two groups of blacks and the outside world. On this issue of impact both from within and from without, Mr. Robinson gave the following illustration:

> . . . The Middle East question obviously has implications for Africa as do most of the questions about which we will be talking in the international arena. It's much the same analysis in reverse that I just made. When you move it from a constituency argument to an issue argument, the issues affect each other as well and we have to have some concern about all of them. There's another thing to be discussed too. We at one point are black Americans with that kind of narrower concern. But more broadly we are citizens of the United States, and we have a duty and a responsibility to participate in the foreign policy. Whoever had the impression that foreign policy was made in a vacuum? Foreign policy is made by people and the people who traditionally made it were the Anglo-Saxon Americans who felt that that was their special preserve. Well, enough of that kind of foolishness. There have always been barriers erected, but we don't accept those barriers. As American citizens we are going to participate fully in this policy. We pay taxes in this country, we die for this country, and we are going to see to it that our views are reflected in the policy that is presented to the world about this country.[85]

On the issue of both national and group identity and loyalty, that is, when it comes to Transafrica's push to support African interests that might be contrary to those of the United States, or, pushing important U.S. issues that might not be in line with those of the Organization of African Unity (OAU), thus resulting in conflicting loyalties, Robinson said:

I don't think so. There's another compass that one can
use. I like to think that we make our determinations on
the basis of what we think is right and fair. We have
assembled here a bunch of people who are largely inspired by various kinds of ideals. They believe in self-
determination, they believe in the same things that the
United States has always claimed to believe in, that the
world community believes in. We believe in economic
and political independence, freedom from minority rule
in southern Africa, and we take them seriously. So using
that kind of compass one doesn't worry so much about
whether it's opposed to U.S. or OAU policies. We have
undertaken a good many policies that are bothersome
to some African countries, favored by others, favored
by this administration, opposed by the administration.
We are not in this business to be ordered about by the
administration or to take instructions from the OAU. We
talk to the OAU; we talk to the African heads of state;
we talk to the administration here; but we independently
make decisions about what we think ought to be done.
On the question of whether or not one is loyal to the
United States, I think this sort of nationalism is destruc-
tive in the final analysis. No one ever questioned whether
those who supported the Marshall Plan in Europe were
loyal to the United States. There has never been a question about the Anglo-American relationships on this
issue of loyalty because there is assumed a compatability
between the United States and Europe. I don't see anything unnatural about the same kind of compatibility between the United States and the Third World and particularly with Africa. So when one talks about America, I ask
whose America? What America? My answer to them, for
those who think that my views are different from theirs
on America, is that I am as American as they. My views
are as legitimately American as theirs. So the question is,
who defines what is the American interest and what is the
American view? We say that our constituency will and
must have a great deal to do with defining that as well,

so I do not see any natural incompatibility between what we would want, what Africa wants, and what the United States wants. The question in the final analysis is what is in the human interest.[86]

As a young black man, Robinson seems to touch upon several major issues that other black predecessors have raised since time immemorial: the need for black people wherever they may be to try and identify, and more importantly, attempt to work with one another. It is interesting to note, too, that some of the questions that plagued most black American movements forging ties with Africa still persist: Is this movement or organization a grassroot one or an elitist one? Would black Americans do better to deal with their own problems here at home rather than getting involved abroad? Who defines black people and what they want and need?[87]

A recent phenomenon that clearly demonstrated black identity and close social relations was the International Festival that took place in February 1977 in Lagos, Nigeria.[88]

Poinsett, outlining forces that attempted to hamper this great event of African reunion, pointed out that "neither British intransigence nor the historical tension between the West and Africa it illustrated, really matter." He indicated that the American press ignored the great black event. Nigeria's fear of "enemy agents" in Lagos seeking to "destroy the unity of Black people" could not stem the rising tide of history. Seventeen thousand black people attended the festivities.[89]

Blacks from the United States, Latin Americans, Australian aborigines, and people from the islands all bowed under the Benin Bronze. "Over it all," Poinsett continued, "was the Mask of Benin Bronze, and a haunting omnipresence mocking those who would divide black people." For the Festival signified that black and African peoples had journeyed to Lagos to confirm and celebrate those cultural and spiritual values that bound them together despite their dispersal around the world. Theirs was also a political mission. For many of them saw their common oppression and exploitation, a malaise reflected in their culture, as the potential basis for a united political front against a common

enemy. Despite their diversity, despite their various lifestyles,
despite their multiple languages, the very coming together of
this vast congregation echoed a common desire to accept themselves as they were, to reject nonblack interpretations of them,
to redefine reality in their own image and regain control of
their destiny. They came to Lagos, declared Festival officials,
"to insure their survival, resurgence, propagation and promo-
tion of Black and African values and civilization."[90]

This great black family reunion demonstrates attempts that
have been made, as well as those being made, for black people
to identify with their cultural and historical origins. The fact
that the Festival took place in 1977, with multitudes of blacks
from all over the world coming together, was a monumental
case of black identity. The next black family reunion, or festival, was slated to take place in Ethiopia in 1981.

In addition to organizations and associations that have contributed greatly to black American and African identifications,
there are individual black Americans and Africans who, in their
own ways, have contributed to the general store of knowledge,
better understanding, and a sense of closer identification between black Americans and Africans.

For example, Alex Haley's search for his own African
ancestry eventually resulted in the bestseller book, *Roots*.[91]
As a result, many black American individuals and groups
found it imperative to journey to Africa in search of their
roots. The television dramatization of *Roots*, shown in
many African nations, awakened many black Africans' sense
of ancestral affinity to blacks in the Diaspora more than ever
before.

Moreover, Andrew Young, the former United States Ambas-
sidor to the United Nations, too provided Africans with one
of the finest examples of what black America could offer:
one of their best and ablest sons, a person loved and trusted,
was to play a major role in the international arena of diplomacy.
Perhaps Andrew Young's contribution to black African and
American relations is illustrated best by Eddie Stone's description of what Americans in general thought and felt about Africa
before and after Andrew Young:

Until the 1960s, the average American citizen regarded
the continent of Africa with a kind of chilling wariness.
It had been called the Dark Continent in books and
films, and the impression most people had of Africa was
one in which the primeval elements ran rampant. Africa
was a primitive place, filled with dark-skinned people who
regularly ate missionaries. The Negroes of Africa, to the
American mind, were a different breed than the American
Negro. Our Negroes, they said, were educated and civilized, and the African Negroes represented the baser state
of being from which the American Negro had "progressed."
To many, the only hope for Africa lay with the colonial
powers that maintained order and civilization in the Dark
Continent.[92]

Stone assessed Young's contributions after his assignment
at the United Nations as follows:

Probably Young's finest contribution to the African situation was his ability to make the American people aware
of what was really going on there. As a nation, we were
exposed to a more rational, less paranoid perspective of
Africa. The situation there is always changing and always
complex. Andy Young was able to show the American
people the African situation through the eyes of the
people themselves; he was able to bring a sense of humanity and understanding to what could have easily been a
cold war nightmare. His ability to deal with human beings
as human beings and not cartoons or puppets being dangled
from strings, allowed the American people to view the
situation humanely, something we had not been able to
do during the war in Vietnam. Andy Young was instrumental in bringing Africa to life for the American people,
in making it a land populated by human beings. To many
people, this was Young's greatest success in his dealings
with Africa.[93]

Although there is no Pan-Africanist advocate in Africa in the
same league as Kwame Nkrumah, Mwalimu Julius K. Nyerere,

the president of Tanzania, has been a vigorous voice encouraging black people from the Diaspora, and especially those with skills, to return home to Tanzania and together help build the nation. The important Sixth Pan-African Conference in Tanzania, which he hosted, help to bring together black people after a long time, cost the government of Tanzania more than a half million dollars, a major outlay for a developing nation.

These events show that black people identify with each other more and more. Black people have come to realize that, as people of color in a white-dominated, hostile world, they share a common identity with one another through their long history of suppression and oppression by white-dominated societies; they have come to define themselves as a class of oppressed peoples, which is inclusive of other nonwhites from the Third World.[94]

They have discovered, through their struggle to free themselves, that they cannot rest, even when their own nations have gained political independence, as long as there still exist pockets of colonized and oppressed people anywhere in the world.[95] They have also discovered that it is not enough for a nation to be politically free if individuals have not yet achieved economic and cultural independence.[96]

Black leaders have tried to foster class struggle and class consciousness among the masses. In opposition, white capitalists have assumed the role of "middlemen," emphasizing differences that they maintain exist among the masses of the world. The Pan-Africanist emphasizes the similarities of their class struggle; they have set out to link up the world of the exploited masses to revolt against the exploiters.[97]

Perhaps what most accurately sums up the new mood in the struggle of black people is a pamphlet by the Pan-African Secretariat for the annual conference held in Georgetown, Guyana, on February 25-28, 1971. This conference resolved to "elicit financial, spiritual, and material aid for the defenders of our homeland. Toward this end, we further resolve to join with Africans and others of the Third World in commemorating World Solidarity Day, May 25." The pamphlet added:

1. We will say to all who will continue to oppress people
   that we, Africans at home and abroad, are united in
   our determination that our homeland shall be free and
   that Africans shall once again be a sovereign people
   and,

2. Will demonstrate to our brothers and sisters at home
   our understanding that their struggle is our struggle
   and that we who have been removed from the land of
   our ancestors, materially as well as spiritually, support
   their heroism.[98]

Black Americans and Africans have sought to maintain relationships with one another and have continued to do so to present times. Looking at the history of the Pan-African Movement
has brought out this point. Blacks in all walks of life, from
both the Old World and the New World, have joined together
in support of African liberation.

It has been demonstrated that blacks as a people have their
own culture, which has been incorporated into the rest of the
world civilization. This culture, it has been noted, has its roots
within the larger continent of Africa.

We shall now turn to examine other blacks to give us a sense
of how they view their world. Unlike the world of science that
views the world from a cold objective stand, we shall look at
black writers, poets, novelists, musicians, dancers, and artists
from other fields to provide us with the emotional point of
view—the flavor of black struggles, pain, tears, longings, and
the excitement of the discovery of love for themselves and
their heritage. The inclusion of these works is central to this
discussion because, as pointed out according to the Afrocentric
view, most strands of distinctive black American "cultural survivals" were manifested poignantly within the black arts. We
shall examine them to see what they have to say about black
American and African identifications. This is important because black students on American campuses generally thrive
on such works. It is this kind of informal background in which
peoples' attitudes towards life are molded.

Notes

1. Miles Mark Fisher, "Deep River." In *Black Brotherhood: Afro-Americans*, ed. Uken Edet Uya (Lexington, Mass.: Heath & Co., 1971), p. 2; Elizabeth Donnan, *Documents Illustrative of the Slave Trade to America*, (Washington, 1930-1935), vol. 2, p. 232n., vol. 3, p. 231; J. S. Buckingham, *American Historical Statistics and Description* (London, 1841), vol. 1, pp. 434, 435; Nancy Price, *A Narrative of Life and Travels of Mrs. Nancy Price* (2nd ed., Boston, 1853).

2. Sierra Leone Company, *Substance of the Report Delivered by the Court of Directors of the Sierra Leone Company, to the General Court of Proprietors, on Thursday, March 27th, 1794* (Philadelphia, 1795), p. 7; J. J. Crooks, *A History of the Colony of Sierra Leone, West Africa* (Dublin, 1906). Sierra Leone had been established as an asylum for Negro British subjects in 1787. Andrew Hull Foote, *Africa and the American Flag* (New York, 1854), p. 77 in Fisher, *passim.*

3. Robert Finley, "Thoughts on Colonizing of Free Blacks" (Washington, 1816).

4. John Briste, *America and Her Resources* (London, 1818), p. 149; John M. Duncan, *Travels Through Part of the United States and Canada in 1818 and 1819* (New York, 1823), vol. 2, p. 261; *Report of the American Colonization Society* (1825), vol. 7, p. 26.

5. Louis Mehlinger, "Attitude of the Free Negro Toward African Colonization," *Journal of Negro History* 1 (July, 1916): 271-301.

6. Hollis R. Lynch, "Pan-Negro Nationalism in the New World, Before 1862," *African History*, ed. Jeffrey Butler (Boston University Press, 1966), vol. 2, pp. 149-79.

7. George Shepperson, "Notes on Negro America Influences on the Emergence of African Nationalism," *Journal of African History* 1, 2 (1960): 301.

8. Alexander Crummell, "Free Coloured Men," p. 73.

9. Ibid.

10. Ibid.

11. Martin H. Delany, *Official Report of the Niger Valley Exploring Party* (1861) 27, Schomburg Collection, New York Public Library.

12. Martin H. Delany, *Official Report of the Niger Valley Exploring Party* (1861) 64, Schomburg Collection, New York Public Library.

13. *Weekly Anglo-American* 1 (September 24, 1859), Schomburg Collection, New York Public Library.

14. Martin H. Delany, *Official Report* 23, Schomburg Collection, New York Public Library.

15. *Weekly Anglo-Africa* 1 (October 1, 1859), Schomburg Collection, New York Public Library.

16. Cited in the *Forty-Sixth Annual Report*, American Colonization Society (Washington, D.C., 1863), p. 6.

17. William E. B. Du Bois, *The Souls of Black Folk* (Chicago: McClurg, 1903).

18. Ibid., p. 70.

19. Ibid., p. 214.

20. Ibid., pp. 241-42.

21. Ibid., p. 215.

22. Ibid.

23. Ibid., p. 342.

24. Richard B. Moore, "Du Bois and Pan-Africa." In *Black Brotherhood: Afro-Americans and Africa*, ed. Uken Edet Uya (Lexington, Mass.: D. C. Heath & Company, 1971), p. 156.

25. Ibid.

26. Clarence G. Contee, *Henry Sylvester Williams and Origins of Organizations Pan-Africanism, 1897-1902.* n.p., n.d., Schomburg Collection, New York Public Library.

27. Ibid., p. 2.

28. Adolf Crabowski, "Tri-Continental Trilogy." In *Time of War*, Schomburg Collection, New York Public Library.

29. Moore, "Du Bois and Pan-Africa," p. 156.

30. Ibid., p. 157.

31. Ibid.

32. For further information concerning the African students who had come to the United States to study, being aided by predominantly black Americans, in black colleges and universities in the United States and the subsequent influences on African political thinking, see George Shepperson, "Notes on Negro American Influences on the Emergence of African Nationalism," *Journal of African History* 1 (1960).

33. Marcus Garvey, *The Tragedy of White Injustice* (New York: Amy Jacques Garvey, 1927), p. 7. Schomburg Collection, New York Public Library.

34. Marcus Garvey Day, "Special African Nationalist Pioneer Movement Newsletter," African Nationalist Pioneer Movement. n.d. Schomburg Collection, New York Public Library.

35. Marcus Garvey, *Philosophy and Opinions of Marcus Garvey* (New York: Universal Publishing House, 1923) vol. 1, p. 7.

36. Ibid.

37. Colin Legum, *Pan-Africanism: A Short Political Guide* (London: Pall Mall Press, 1962), p. 25.

38. For the complete list of demands by the Third Conference, see W. E. B. Du Bois, *The World and Africa* (New York: International Publishers, 1946), p. 242.

39. There is a conflict in sequence of the Fourth Congress. While Du Bois as well as the American Women Pamphlet both list the 1927 Conference in New York as the Fourth Congress, Moore lists this date and Congress as the Fifth Congress. See Du Bois, *The World and Africa*, pp. 242-243, and Moore, "Du Bois and Pan-Africa," p. 167. Also the Negro Women's Pamphlet. Moore indicates that the Fourth Congress met in 1923, weekly in London and in Lisbon. See Moore, p. 166.

40. Pan-African Congress *Bulletin 1*, compiled by Public Committee Circle for Peace and Foreign Relations, August 21-24, 1927, Schomburg Collection, New York Public Library.

41. *New York Amsterdam News* (August 24, 1924). Schomburg Collection, New York Public Library.

42. Ibid.

43. Frances E. Lewis, *Guardian* (August 27, 1924). Schomburg Collection, New York Public Library.

44. *The Chicago Bee*, "Pan-African Congress Public Manifesto," September 3, 1927. Schomburg Collection, New York Public Library.

45. For this Congress, the dates and places of Du Bois and Moore coincide. However, Du Bois lists it as the Fifth Conference while Moore lists it as the Sixth. See Du Bois, *The World and Africa*, pp. 167-68.

46. Moore, "Du Bois and Pan-Africa," p. 168.

47. Ibid., pp. 169-170.

48. C. Eric Lincoln, "Mood Ebony: The Acceptance of Being Black." In *Old Memories, New Moods*, ed. Peter Z. Rose (New York: Atherton Press, Inc., 1970), p. 367.

49. Ibid.

50. Ibid., p. 368.

51. Ibid.

52. Kwame Nkrumah, quoted in Richard B. Moore, "Du Bois and Pan-Africa," p. 164.

53. Melville J. Herskovits, *The Myth of the Negro Past* (New York: Harper and Row, 1941).

54. Nathan Hare, "A Radical Perspective on Social Science Curricula." In *Black Studies in the University: A Symposium* ed. Armstead L. Robinson, et al. (New Haven, Conn.: Yale University Press, 1969), pp. 108-9.

55. Melville J. Herskovits, "What Has Africa Given America?" *New Republic* 1083: 92-94.

56. Melville J. Herskovits, "The Present Status and Needs of Afro-

American Research," *Journal of Negro History* 36 (2): 123-47.
    57. Erika E. Bourguignon, "Religious Syncretism among New World
Negroes." Papers presented to the American Anthropological Association.
(Quoted in Introduction: "Ritual Dissociation and Possession Belief in
Caribbean Negro Religion." In *Afro-American Anthropology: Contemporary Perspectives*, ed. Norman E. Whitten and John F. Szwed (New
York: Macmillan, 1970a). "Afro-American Regions Traditions and
Transformation." In *Black America*, ed. John F. Szwed (New York:
Basic Books, 1970b).
    58. John F. Szwed, "Afro-American Musical Adaptation." In *Afro-American Anthropology*, ed. Whitten and Szwed.
    59. Norman E. Whitten, "Personal Networks and Musical Contexts
in the Pacific Lowlands of Colombia and Equador." In *Afro-American
Anthropology*, ed. Whitten and Szwed.
    60. Alan Lomax, "The Homogeneity of Afro-American Musical Style."
In *Afro-American Anthropology*, ed. Whitten and Szwed.
    61. Daniel J. Crowley, "African Folktales in Afro-America." In *Black
America*, ed. Szwed.
    62. Wright, Richard, "Blueprint for Negro Literature," *New Challenge*,
1937. New version in *Amistad 2*, ed. John A. Williams and Charles F.
Harris (New York: Random House, 1971), pp. 5-6.
    63. Ibid., p. 20.
    64. George Shepperson, "Notes on Negro American Influences on the
Emergence of African Nationalism," *Journal of African History* 1, 2
(1960).
    65. Ralph Ellison, *Shadow and Act* (New York: Random House,
1964), p. 271.
    66. Eldridge Cleaver, *Post-Prison Writings and Speeches* (New York:
Random House, 1968), p. 75.
    67. Vincent Harding, "Beyond Chaos: Black History and the Search
for the New Land." In *Amistad*, ed. John A. Williams and Charles F.
Harris (New York: Random House, 1970), p. 279.
    68. Arthur L. Smith, *Language, Communication, and Rhetoric in
Black America* (New York: Harper and Row, Publishers, 1972), p. x.
    69. LeRoi Jones, *Blues People: The Negro Experience in White America and the Music That Developed from It* (New York: William Morrow
and Company, 1963), p. 25.
    70. Harold Cruse, *The Crisis of the Negro Intellectual: From Its Origins
to the Present* (New York: William Morrow and Company, Inc., 1967),
p. 38.
    71. *The Black Bulletin*, Schomburg Collection, New York Public
Library (n.d.), p. 1.

72. African Heritage Studies Association, Schomburg Collection, New York Public Library.

73. *The Black Bulletin: Black Nationalist Newsletter.* Schomburg Collection, New York Public Library, p. x.

74. Alma Robinson, "Sixth Pan-African Conference Africa and Afro-American" in *Africa Report* 19 (September-October 1974): 7-10.

75. Ibid., p. 9.

76. Ibid., pp. 8-9.

77. Ibid., p. 8.

78. Ibid., p. 10.

79. Anthony J. Hughes, "Interview" with Randall Robinson, Executive Director, Transafrica. In *Africa Report* 25, 1, (January-February 1980), pp. 9-15.

80. Ibid., p. 9.

81. Ibid.

82. Ibid.

83. Ibid.

84. Ibid.

85. Ibid., pp. 9-10.

86. Ibid., p. 10.

87. Ibid., pp. 10-11.

88. Alex Poinsett, "Festac '77: Festival in Nigeria Strengthens Bond Between Black-American and Africa," *Ebony* 32, 7 (May 1977): 33.

89. Ibid., p. 33.

90. Ibid., p. 40.

91. Alex Haley, *Roots* (New York: Doubleday and Co., 1976).

92. Eddie Stone, *Andrew Young: Biography of a Realist,* (Los Angeles: Holloway House Publishing Co. 1980), p. 123.

93. Ibid., p. 131.

94. Frantz Fanon, *The Wretched of the Earth* (New York: Grove Press, 1966), and Fanon, *Black Skin, White Masks* (New York: Grove Press, 1967).

95. Eldridge Cleaver, *Soul on Ice* (New York: Dell, 1968), *Post-Prison Writings and Speeches, On Ideology of the Black Panther Party* (San Francisco: Black Panther Party, 1970).

96. Stokely Carmichael and Charles Hamilton, *Black Power: The Politics of Liberation in America* (New York: Vintage Books, 1968).

97. William E. B. Du Bois, *The World and Africa* (New York: Harcourt Brace, 1935).

98. Kwayana Eusi, (Coordinating Elder), "Brothers and Sisters," Pan-African Secretariat, 1971. Schomburg Collection, New York Public Library.

3.
Literary Views
_____ # of Black Culture

This chapter reviews works of literary figures from Africa, the United States, and the Caribbean islands. It is essential to look at these works for several reasons. First, the literary artistic work provides us with a cultural "red-thread" that connects the work of the social scientists and activists with the subjective. For in these works we get emotion, tone, rhythm, quality, feel, and much more not easily subject to rigorous scientific quantification. Second, in these works we find a "deliberate" attempt to define, in their own unique ways, what the artists feel is African culture, who Africans are, and, above all, what Africa is. Third, these writers are from both Africa and the Diaspora. More important, they all have in common the fact that they have in one way or another participated fully within the Western way of life but have, to one degree or another, been rejected by the Western, predominantly white world and have in turn decided to reject it, either in full or partially. Eric Lincoln has stated: "They want to be black men because they were rejected by white men. And they bought a dream in Africa because, in the American dream, they always woke up screaming."[1] Fourth, this cultural background has influenced the students, whether they have or have not read these authors. Some who rejected the Western way of life have chosen to reconstruct "the African way" of life as it was practiced during the precolonial days. Others insist that going back to African cultural roots would be impractical and opt to follow Western trains of thought. Others feel that a sort of synthesis has to be reached whereby some African cultural patterns and practices can be adapted and adopted and mixed with the Western to form a synthesis, a sort of neo-African culture. We shall now turn to examine what they have to say themselves.

In the 1920s in Harlem a black literary and artistic expression came into vogue. This potent movement became known as the "Negro Renaissance."

The Negro Renaissance was a crystallization of philosophical differences that existed between two major black leaders, W. E. B. Du Bois and Booker T. Washington, with regard to black peoples' freedom and education. Washington once had declared "the agitation of questions of social equality is the extremest folly."[2] For Washington felt that "in all things that are purely social we can be as separate as the fingers, yet one as the hand in all things essential to mutual progress." According to Washington critics, including Du Bois, he had renounced the black peoples' political struggle, higher education, and civil rights guaranteed under the American Constitution. The critics felt that Washington had not only acknowledged the inferiority of blacks, but had accepted it!

Du Bois, on the other hand, was viewed as a man seeking political equality of the races as well as encouraging higher educational attainment for blacks, though only for those he conceded to be his "talented tenth." In 1910, he founded the National Association for the Advancement of Colored People (NAACP) as a lobbying tool to defend black rights mainly through legal channels, as well as the magazine *Crisis.*

Black writing that emerged during this era has been characterized as "protest writing." Protesting assimilation into the American mainstream has often been referred to as "exotic," along with the proletarian anti-bourgeois identification with African cultural roots. Langston Hughes wrote a poem in 1922 that appeared in *Crisis* in which he clearly identified himself with his Africa:

> I am a Negro
>> Black as the night is black,
>> Black like the depths of my Africa: . . .

I've been a singer:
  All the way from Africa to Georgia I
    carried my sorrow song
  I made ragtime

I've been a victim:
  The Belgian cut off my hands in the Congo.
  They lynch me now in Texas.[3]

Or when he reacted to Western civilization, he wrote:

I am afraid of this civilization
  so hard, so strong, so cold . . .[4]

Of his longing for Africa, Hughes wrote in 1931:

So long,
So far away
Is Africa.
Not even memories alive
. . . Save those that songs
Beat back into the blood.[5]

Thus, black Americans' longing and yearning for Africa and for their African cultural roots as reflected by a few black intellectuals came into the foreground. Blacks in America were no longer ashamed to expound their blackness or their African origins. They wanted to know who they were and where they came from. Harlem became a potent black cultural, artistic, and literary center, and even the most sophisticated white patrons left their secluded homes on Park Avenue and headed for Harlem to enjoy black cultural experiences they had never thought existed before. It was as if whites were discovering for the first time that blacks existed.

In 1934 in Paris, a black literary movement was born when a few students founded *L'Etudiant Noir*. The work that was produced between 1934 and 1948 came to be known as *Negritude*. Those who wrote in this mode combined political fervor with their passion for African culture. As Sedar Senghor once remarked: "For us politics was only an aspect of culture," and then added, "we accepted surrealism as a means but not as an end, as an ally not as a master. We are willing to find inspiration in surrealism, but solely because surrealistic writing rediscovered the language of Negro Africa."[6]

Surrealism as a form and style of literary expression has been described by Jahn as a modern movement in art and literature in which an attempt is made to portray the workings of the subconscious mind, as by arranging material in unexpected fantastic ways. As surrealism was associated with Western forms of artistic expressions, the Negritude critics maintained that, if Africans were going to bring forth a different form of expression, they had to come up with something new, something characteristically African. The Negritude response was that unique African expressions can, indeed, be portrayed through surrealism without necessarily losing their being and special qualities. As Senghor pointed out, it is only a vehicle to arrive at the end.[7]

Aimé Césaire, defending the style of black writers' authenticity, said:

> The ordinary Negro, whose grotesqueness or eroticism a whole literature sets out to emphasize, is made a hero, drawn seriously and passionately, and the limited power of his art is successful. . . . To create a world, is that a small thing? To make a world emerge where only the junk-shop's exotic inhumanity rose before?[8]

These writers, in so many ways, were trying to define their own being distinct from that of negative stereotyped Western tradition. They were trying to build it bit by bit without the benefit of a long tradition behind them. Critics who emerged to attack this viable literary movement viewed it skeptically and, in some cases, searched for a way to fit it somewhere neatly within the framework of already-established literary works. Black writers reacted by asserting that Negritude is the black peoples' "being in the world" or that it is . . . "the rhythm born of emotion." Sartre joined black writers to proclaim: "Negritude, in contrast, is understanding through sympathy." Senghor added: "It is the same independence as with Negritude. This is first of all a *negation* . . . rejection of the other, refusal to assimilate . . . rejection of other is self-affirmation." Or, viewing it as a skin color, Césaire said: "His very negritude was losing its color." Senghor summed it up as "Negritude is the cultural heritage, values, and above all the *spirit* of the Negro-African civilization" and "Negritude, the *sum* of Black Africans' cultural values."⁹

Black artists as well as intellectuals were trying to define this unique blackness and their cultural creations. Some like Senghor called it Negritude, or being African; others called it "African personality." The central question still remained whether black intellectuals were going to remain drowned within assimilation to Westernism or whether they were going to replace it with something uniquely their own.

Assimilation is totally rejected by Alioune Diop as a type of relationship inspired by colonialism. On this he said:

> Its aim is to make the individual (it is never concerned with anything but individuals), torn from the background natural to him and which brought out his *own personality*, agree to replace his habits of thinking, feeling and acting by others, which he could only share with an alien community . . . our peoples reject assimilation without at the same time wishing to isolate themselves in their own cultures. They thought choice between isolation and assimilation has during the last ten years been the trap in which the malice of the colonizer has cunningly tried to catch the conscience of the Africans. But life is not simple. It is true that there is another trap, which consists of innocently putting you to the challenge of choosing which African values to preserve and which European values to adopt. . . . the men of culture of the Negro world do not disguise from themselves in the magnitude of their responsibility as the link between the western world and the universe of their peoples. They have certain responsibilities in purifying the morals of the language of the

culture which the west tends to impose upon the whole planet. . . . In the face of that culture our role in the immediate future must be to redress all the errors and false values introduced and turned into institutions in Europe by a unilaterally creative subjectivity, whose passionate urge was given tenfold strength by the whole weight of European imperialism.[10] [emphasis added]

Diop was trying to challenge his colleagues to redress all errors and false values imposed by Europeans' "unilateral creative subjectivity." If the Europeans have erred in treating the African cultural past, then blacks themselves must take on the heavy responsibility of correcting them. The "African personality" must come through as defined by black people themselves.

What then is this "African personality" or "Negritude" that Diop was talking about? Is it something unique, different from all other forms of personalities? Let us look at how it has been used by blacks in other fields.

In economic terms, for example, Sékou Touré says it must be the responsibility of Africans to:

> . . . rediscover its *African personality:* with regard to law, that it must be worked out on the basis of "the *African personality*" of education, that its mission is "the rehabilitation and blossoming of the *African personality.*" Always the same word, always the same fundamental requirement, Africans and the same endeavor to dislodge the "spirit of singularity" in all places at the same time.[11]

The historical interpretation of the "African personality" was viewed by Kwame Nkrumah in his address to the First Conference of Independent African States. He said:

> For too long in our history, Africa has spoken through the voice of others. Now, what I have called an *African personality* in international affairs will have a chance of making a proper impact through the voices of Africa's own sons.[12] [emphasis added]

Tom Mboya, of Kenya, viewed "African personality" in cul-
turistic terms when he said:

> The *"African personality"* would be meaningless if it were
> to be identified with the noble things Africa fought for. . . .
> She has a clean past and a new start, and instead of joining
> any of the present power blocs or forming just another
> bloc, she should concentrate on establishing her own *per-
> sonality* in the context of dedication to basic individual
> freedoms and civil liberties.[13] [emphasis added]

To Diop, African personality is "humanism" as defined when
he said:

> The African personality, which is the basis and founda-
> tion of our humanism, aspires . . . to being freed from
> the Western grip. *It requires that our people should speak
> through us* . . . Our peoples only mean to give expression
> to what they alone can show forth: how they see them-
> selves, how they identify themselves in the context of the
> world situation and of the great problems of mankind.[14]
> [emphasis added]

The concept of Negritude or "African personality" is the
black intellectuals' way of expressing themselves and their world,
as has been aptly projected by Jahn, who summed it up as
follows:

> (Negritude). In connection with this view of the world,
> the African writer has a very important function: he is
> word-magician and announcer, African spokesman,
> sponsor and interpreter to the outside world, Africa's
> educator within. His rhythmical word produces the images
> which when put together become poetry and prose. Reality
> offers dormant poetry and prose. Reality offers dormant
> subject matter, which his awakens, turns into images and
> projects toward the future. The functions of this kind of
> writing is not to describe things as they are for the sake
> of description, but to create prototypes: visions of what

ought to be. Therefore, the style is "in imperative." When
the writer transposes his vision of the future into the
present, or even back into the past, as if what he com-
manded were taking place before his eyes or as if the new
reality invoked had already come into being, his imperative achieves its highest force.[15]

Senghor does not hesitate to say where the origins of this
special quality come from, e.g., "The millenium of his tropical
experience and the agricultural nature of his existence; the heat
and humidity of tropical regions and a pastoral closeness to
the earth, and the rhythms of its seasons." "Emotion," he finds,
"is at the heart of Negritude." For, he proclaims, "emotion is
Negro."[16]

Samuel Allen, the Negro poet, in his attempt to analyze the
concept of Negritude as presented by Aimé Césaire and Leopold
Senghor, as well as in Sartre's interpretation, sums it up by
agreeing with Alioune Diop, Secretary of the Paris-born
Society of African Culture, that Negritude "gives as a raison
d'être of a Negritude the fact that the world has been taught
there is no culture other than the West's, no universal value
which has only begun to reshape this image of man upon the
earth. Negritude, then, is the complete ensemble of values of
African culture, and the vindication of the dignity of persons
of African descent."[17]

Fanon, who went full circle from being totally assimilated
to French culture to his final metamorphosis into a black protest writer who knew the French thoroughly, said:

> In this poetry I have found not only my situation, but
> *myself.* I feel in myself a soul as large as the world, a
> soul as deep as the deepest rivers, my breast swells to in-
> finity. And then they recommend to me the modesty of
> a sick man. Irresponsible, mounted between nothing and
> the infinite, I begin to weep.[18]

Among many black literary figures who expounded the concept of Negritude as being African, culturally going back to its

original roots and giving it a special quality distinctive from all others, were those who did not feel the same about Negritude.

Wole Soyinka, reacting to Senghor's Negritude, retorted: "I don't think a tiger has to go around proclaiming his tigritude; he pounces." That is, blacks do not need to go around proclaiming their blackness or the fact that they have something special and unique. They are black, they know it, and everybody else ought to know it. He continued:

> In other words: a tiger does not stand in the forest and say: I am a tiger. When you pass where a tiger has walked before, you see the skeleton of the duiker, you know that some *tigritude* has been emanated there. . . . I was trying to distinguish between propaganda and true poetic creativity. I was saying in other words that what one expected from poetry was an intrinsic poetic quality, not a name-dropping.[19] [emphasis added]

Gerald Moore, reacting to Soyinka's attitude, said, "this attitude is a trifle unfair,"[20] whereas Ezekiel Mphahlele, a South African writer, said that there is no such thing as Negritude, "as being African." The result, says Jahn, "has been violent arguments between French-writing and English-writing African authors, on the 'emotion,' as it were, of 'Tigritude versus Negritude.' "[21]

If the Tigritude school does not find it practical to go back into the African past and find what it means to be "African," what then do they suggest?

Ezekiel Mphahlele says:

> It seems to me, an outsider, that the Negro commitment is so huge in his country that he will probably find it more profitable to concern himself with producing good art inside his social climate, as a "native son." If he finds the American civilization frustrating, he should realize that it is not a parochial malady. Everywhere, especially in Africa, we are up against this invasion by the white world upon our senses of values.[22]

Mphahlele feels that the sense of frustration in America is not unique but rather a universal phenomenon shared by people with similar experiences. He adds that:

> Our music, dancing, writing and other arts reveal the cultural cross-impacts that have so much influenced our lives over the last three hundred years and *Negritude* to us is just so much airy intellectual talk either in terms of artistic activity or as a fighting faith. It is exciting, even if my writing is often excruciating, to be the meeting point of different cultural streams. If my writing shows any Africanness, it is as it should be, if my note and tone has an authenticity. I take my Negroness for granted, and it is no matter for slogans. Imagine a Chinaman waking up one morning and shouting in the streets that he has discovered something Chinese in his sculpture or painting or music.[23]

He even thought it "phoney" when he heard that Senghor's poetry, written in French, was read being accompanied by African drums, "because the rhythm of drums is just not the rhythm of French poetry."

But David Rubadiri announced: "I think that Negritude is dangerous . . . because its final result is to press down the creative spirit, to tie it. Sometimes so tight that a work of art becomes meaningless." To emphasize his point, he added further that "when you come to think of it, any self-respecting nudist of any race could declare this."[24]

Among some black American writers the concept of Negritude or going-back-to-African roots evoked mixed responses just as among Africans.

Ralph Ellison said, "African content of American Negro life is more fanciful than actual." Commenting on his African roots he said:

> I answer that I am a Negro American. . . . For me, the Negro is a member of an American-bound cultural group with its own idiom, its own psychology. The American

Negro stock is here, a synthesis of various African cultures, then of slavery, and of all the experiences of Negro since.[25]

Lorraine Hansberry felt that she was not "African or Mexican" but from "Chicago and New York." "Africans," she once said, "have their own identities and American Negroes have—or must shape—their own."[26]

James Baldwin summed it up in: "this depthless alienation from oneself and one's people is, in sum, the American experience." Going back to African cultural roots seemed to have eluded him after meeting some African students in Paris. Then, he concluded, he had not

> . . . endured the utter alienation of himself from his people and his past. His mother did not sing "Sometimes I feel like a motherless child." . . . They face each other, the Negro and the African, over a gulf of three hundred years—an alienation too vast to be conquered in an evening of good will. . . .[27]

Then there are those enterprising writers who want to go it alone as individuals. As Brown says, "the integration of the Negro artist means his acceptance as an individual to be judged on his own merit, with no favors granted and no fault found because of his race."[28]

Sedar Senghor, reacting to Aimé Césaire's qualitative choice from both cultures, had this to say:

> Césaire is right when he says—and I said it myself twenty years ago—that we must not be assimilated, we must assimilate, that is, there must be freedom of choice, there must be freedom of assimilation . . . even when we have solved this problem (of colonialism), there will still be another problem—that of choice between civilization in contact, we shall have to see what we shall keep from Negro African civilization.[29]

The black writers characterized here seem to want to be free to participate in both cultures like a Chinese cultural menu;

they want to pick and choose, to adapt and adopt cultural patterns from both cultures. They do not feel that one can work with only one form, as they are a product of both cultures. This attitude was beautifully summed up by Jahn when he wrote about black writers:

> . . . African intelligence wants to integrate into modern life what seems valuable from the past. The goal is neither the traditional African nor the black European but the modern African. This means that a tradition seen rationally whose values are made explicit and renewed, must assimilate those European elements which modern times demand, and in this process the European elements are so transformed and adopted that a modern, viable *African* culture arises out of the whole. It is a question, therefore, of a genuine renewal and limitation of the past, but permits something new to emerge. This something new is already at hand; we call it neo-African culture.[30]

What has clearly emerged so far in this chapter has been a healthy debate among black writers, politicians, activists, and others on how they view and define themselves and their black world. It has become fairly evident that they are struggling to make sense out of a rather mixed-up cultural world. Keeping in mind the two premises already discussed, the Eurocentric view and the Afrocentric view, the same themes seem to characterize these writers; that is, they view black identity and social relationships through either a Eurocentric or an Afrocentric perspective.

Although black people express themselves in diverse ways, they seem to agree that there is something uniquely African that needs to be expressed. Where the difference of opinion seems to crystallize is, in effect, whether or not this unique African "Negritude" or "personality" should be exercised or taken for granted.

Writers such as Senghor, Hughes, Césaire, and Diop seem to share the same philosophical outlook toward the study of African cultural expression as those discussed in Chapter 2 on the Afrocentric perspective toward black identity and relations.

Writers such as Soyinka, Mphahlele, Rubadiri, Ellison, Hansberry, and Baldwin seem to feel that though black people are related, nonetheless each group should work within its own cultural (African or American) milieu. This group of writers could be identified to a certain extent with the Eurocentric view, though there are certain features that clearly set them apart from the Eurocentric view of black relations such as their agreement that blacks have distinctive cultural creations of their own. Whereas Baldwin, Hansberry, and Wright point out that they are Americans of African descent, Soyinka and Mphahlele, black Africans, recognize their African origins but do not find it necessary to demonstrate them to the world; they would rather just be.

From these writers another philosophy on black identity and relations has emerged, the philosophy that has been called "Tigritude," for lack of a better term. Central to this thesis are two distinctive perspectives that characterize and interpret black identity and relationships. The Eurocentric view denies the existence of distinctive cultural creations and black American and African relations. Or, if relations are discovered to exist, they are viewed as "strained." The Afrocentric perspective on black identity and relations holds that blacks have distinctive cultural creations of their own and that black American and African identification exists. What is the balance between Western culture, on the one hand, and African, on the other?

The third philosophy of black relations that has emerged here holds a middle ground, that is, those who would not choose between the Western and the African, but would rather choose the qualitatively best of both worlds and discard the bad from both, a Tigritude view. Within this perspective are Césaire, Brown, and Jahn. They want a synthesis of both cultures. We shall deal with this perspective in detail later on.

If the black literary figures, philosophers, and guardians of their cultural creations do not agree with one another, does that imply that they do not identify with one another? The literature so far examined does not seem to point to this train of thought but rather indicates that they do agree concerning their ends. What seems to be at issue is the means to those ends.

Let us now turn to examine the views of young and up-coming black American and African students on American campuses to see how they define themselves and their world. We shall find out from our next chapter whether or not these young blacks view their identifications and relationships through a Eurocentric, an Afrocentric, or a middle-ground perspective, Tigritude.

Notes

1. Eric Lincoln, "Mood Ebony: The Acceptance of Being Black." In *Americans from Africa: Old Memories, New Moods*, ed. Peter I. Rose (New York: Atherton Press, Inc., 1970), p. 366.

2. Emma L. Thornbrough, ed., *Booker T. Washington* (Englewood Cliffs, N.J.: Prentice-Hall, 1969).

3. Langston Hughes, *The Book of Negro Folklore* (New York: Dodd, Mead, 1959), p. 8.

4. Langston Hughes, *The Weary Blues* (New York: Dodd, Mead, 1926), p. 102.

5. Hughes, *Book of Negro Folklore*, p. 3.

6. Sedar Senghor, in *Les escrivains de langue Française, naissance d'une litterature*, Lilyan Kesteloot (Brussels: Kesteloot, 1963).

7. Ibid.

8. Aimé Césaire, in the *Journal Propique* 2, Forte-de-France, Martinique (July 1941): 41ff.

9. Jahneinz Jahn, *Neo-African Literature: A History of Black Writing* (New York: Grove Press, Inc., 1968), pp. 251-52.

10. Aliune Diop, Opening Address to First Congress of Negro Writers and Artists (Paris: *Présence Africaine* 8, 9, 10 (1956).

11. Sékou Touré, quoted in *Pan-Africanism: A Short Political Guide*, Colin Legum (London: Pall Mall Press, 1962), p. 118.

12. Kwame Nkrumah, in ibid., p. 118.

13. Thomas Joseph Mboya, in ibid., p. 118.

14. Alioune Diop, Opening Speech at the Second Congress of Negro Writers and Artists, Rome, 1960. Quoted in *Legum* (1962): 118.

15. Jahn, *Neo-African Literature*, pp. 251-52.

16. Ibid., p. 250.

17. Samuel Allen, quoted in *The African Image*, Ezekiel Mphahlele (New York: Praeger Paperbacks, 1968), p. 49.

18. Frantz Fanon, *Black Skins, White Masks* (New York: Grove Press, 1967), p. 14.

19. Wole Soyinka, in *Neo-African Literature: A History of Black Writing*, ed. Janheinz Jahn (New York: Grove Press, 1968), p. 266.

20. Ibid.

21. Ezekiel Mphahlele, *The African Image* (New York: Praeger Paperbacks, 1968), p. 52.

22. Ibid.

23. Ezekiel Mphahlele, *Encounter* (London, March, 1961).

24. David Rubadiri, "Why African Literature?" In *Transition*, 4, 15 (Kampala, 1964): p. 41.

25. Mphahlele, *African Image*, p. 47.

26. Ibid.

27. Ibid., p. 48.

28. Ibid.

29. Leopold Sedar Senghor, Discussion at the First Congress of Black Writers and Artists, *Présence Africaine* 8, 9, 10 (1956): 5.

30. Janheinz Jahn, *Muntu* (New York: Grove Press, 1961), p. 16.

4.
The Dimensions of Black American and African ___ Student Relationships

During the 1960s, the world was undergoing drastic changes. Most Third World nations had become or were becoming independent of their former colonizers. The United States and the Soviet Union were trying to put their men on the moon. On the educational front in the United States, many institutions of learning finally had opened their doors to blacks in relatively large numbers. During the 1960s about 200,000 black students were attending college, and by 1970 this number had more than doubled.[1] Formerly black students in higher education more often than not attended predominantly black colleges and universities. In the 1960s, however, institutions that had been exclusively white made deliberate, though reluctant, efforts to recruit black students, including those from lower social classes. During this time, for example, many East African students were brought to America to study through what was known as the "Kennedy Student Airlift" in America or as the "Tom Mboya Student Airlift" in eastern Africa. It is perhaps ironic that in some cases Africans were admitted to these institutions of learning much earlier than black Americans.

Though unconscionable racist acts were perpetrated upon black American students, officially the African students were often given better treatment. But in reality, most American communities accorded African students the same treatment they felt suitable for blacks in general, discriminated against in housing, jobs, choice of schools, and in their social life in general. While black American students met the same fate, it was not new to them; they had known racial discrimination and prejudice all their lives. The Africans, on the other hand, were often at a loss to understand what was happening to them. This common fate of African and black American students on white campuses may have prompted their views of each other to change drastically.

Some black students spoke of the problems of discrimination in a global perspective: they saw and defined the black ghettoes as a "colonial situation" in the generic sense of the words of Frantz Fanon, Malcolm X, Stokely Carmichael, and others, to name just a few of those outspoken blacks who likened the plight of blacks in America to the colonialism and imperialism suffered in Africa and other parts of the Third World.

In the late 1960s and early 1970s, black American students demanded the introduction and teaching of Afro-American studies in their respective colleges and universities, in order to learn of the contributions to world history and civilization made by blacks throughout civilization. They studied revolutionary organizations of other countries, the writings of Frantz Fanon, and the activities of the Black Moslems and particularly of the Black Panthers, who helped to raise their common consciousness. African students were viewed as part of the world struggle of the Third World peoples. Black liberation took on a global meaning; it was not confined within the perimeters of the United States. These events helped shape the common consciousness of black American and African students, melted the two together, and created a mutual affinity for each other's problems.

In analyzing and interpreting this study's data, the responses from the individuals interviewed and surveyed are important insofar as they shed light upon the nature and extent of the changing patterns of social relationships among American and African blacks on an American campus. Individual responses are treated as manifestations of identification of individuals who have been influenced by some, if not most, of the ideas basic to the literature already surveyed.

Analysis and Interpretation of Data

Both black American and African students were asked: "Do you feel you have anything in common with black Americans or Africans?" (See Table 1.) Data indicated that all black

TABLE 1

Respondents' Feelings about Things They Have in Common

Responses	Black Americans		Black Africans	
	Number	Percentage	Number	Percentage
Have things in common	39	98	40	100
Have nothing in common	1*	2	0	0
Total	40	100	40	100

*The one black American respondent who felt he had nothing in common with Africans was of Spanish-African descent; he traced his identity to Spain rather than to Africa.

Africans and all but one black American respondent said that they certainly felt they had many things in common with each other. It is apparent in this study that black people from different continents felt a closer affinity to one another, an Afrocentric view of identity. The explanation for this is several-fold. First, it is the product of a world technological economy in which peoples are coming closer and closer together. Second, it is a factor of an increased awareness of each other's condition and a mutual feeling of frustration at being forced to participate in what is essentially a Western-oriented world economic system in which they have had little input and in which they exercise even less control. Third, a common bond is being forged to give identity and an expression of purpose. Though the two groups of students can be considered academically privileged they, like other students, identify themselves with the low social-economic groups.

To see the effects of this system and its influences upon individual social relationships, it is necessary to examine individual responses. When the respondents from both groups were asked to indicate those things they felt they had in common with one another, interesting patterns emerged: twice as many black African students said that "color and ancestry" is the one dimension of affinity that they felt they shared with their black American brothers and sisters. However, a higher proportion of black American respondents felt that they had external dimensions of identity in common with their African counterparts. Before we proceed further, we should clarify the concepts used.

First, the concept of *internal dimension* of identity means here those internal or inherent attributes that come about through genetic constitution. The individual has no choice or control concerning these attributes as given. Such attributes as color and ancestry fall under this classification. This dimension of identity is important because it has been indicated by a survey of literature that black Americans and Africans have been viewed as biologically related only in terms of internal dimensions of identity. A second dimension of identity as conceived in this study involves *external dimension* of identity, that is, those attributes or relatedness based upon external attributes or forces: elements such as political, social, economic, and cultural aspects all fall under this classification. The relationships between black-American and African students explored in this study will depend upon those elements that are shared.

To show how black Americans and Africans feel about what they have in common with one another, here are some of their responses. First, black Americans expressing *internal dimensions* of identity said:

> I am Black and they are Black. I love them as Black people.
>
> First, they are Blacks in Africa and in America we are all Blacks, therefore we are one people.
>
> We are both of the same ancestral backgrounds.

The main thing we have in common is our ancestral origins as a race of people, and that originates in Africa.

Black Americans expressed also *external dimensions* of identity:

We are oppressed by the same oppressors who are the White society.

I think we both suffer in some form or manner from White racism.

We all should unite and be against the White supremacy and the structures they have erected throughout the world.

I have an interest in cultural backgrounds and their involvements which are capable or equal to our status. I love their culture.

Because we have been both deprived of our own Black identity, I share with them a strong sense of brotherhood. I realize that the language, customs, and other differences were not originally our choice nor was it theirs. I am aware that all problems that we all face, them and me, such as racism in the United States, in South Africa, are all the same and that unity is the best means to deal with it.

Black Africans saw as *internal dimension* of identity:

Our Blackness.

Being Black.

Being Black, we experience the same prejudices.

Racial issues.

Both I and Black-Americans share common characteristics (our Blackness).

Black Africans gave as *external dimensions* of identity:

We have in common our cultural and economic domination by Whites. I guess they are overpowering in every way possible by racist White cultures.

Both of us are struggling for political and economic power.

Colonialization, political problems, views of international affairs.

To me, the fact that these people came here 400 years ago sounds incredible. They behave as 400-year-olds in this country, so I still think their basic culture and way of behavior is well pronounced—African.

Of interest here are two major factors: (1) All the respondents, both black Americans and Africans, indicate that they do feel that they have some things in common with one another. (2) The data indicate, in a ratio of three to one, that black Africans and black Americans respectively perceived their common identity as based upon color and ancestry, an internal dimension. The majority of American respondents felt that they shared an affinity with their African brothers and sisters based upon their common "oppression/suppression" by white people, an external dimension of identity. This is certainly an Afrocentric view.

A second question that emerges here is: Why do two groups of black people perceive their common affinity as based upon two different dimensions of identity? It may be that, as Africans are aware of coming from independent African states, a factor of some psychological and cultural importance, they are less likely to identify themselves along the external dimension of identity. However, as black Americans seem to feel a greater sense of powerlessness from operating within an American system dominated primarily by whites, they are more likely to relate along "oppression/suppression" characteristics of the external dimension of identity.

Though the dimensions of identity have been conceptualized this way, our major concern is not whether the respondents find common identity based upon one or the other of these two dimensions of identity but rather whether the respondents find or do not find common identity at all. The major dimensions of identity help us only to understand the dynamics of the basis of their attribution.

Black Americans' Identification with Africa and Africans

The issue raised in earlier chapters of the basis of identity that black people perceive as having in common is also reflected among the present respondents. For example, black Americans and Africans were asked to state their views as to how black Americans should identify themselves. Four choices were provided: Africa, black America, mutual reciprocity, and each to his own. Some interesting patterns emerge. (See Table 2.)

TABLE 2

Respondents Who Think It Important That Black Americans Attempt to Become Identified with

Choices (with)	Black Americans		Black Africans	
	Number	Percentage	Number	Percentage
Africa	26	65	34	85
Black America	7	18	5	13
Mutual reciprocity	6	15	1	2
Each to his own	1	2	0	0
Total	40	100	40	100

Sixty-five percent of the black American respondents said that black Americans should definitely identify themselves with "Africa." Only a small number of respondents from both groups, 18 percent black American and 13 percent African, felt that black Americans should be identified with "Black America." Fifteen percent of the black Americans and only three percent of the Africans indicated that both groups should have a "mutually reciprocal" relationship of affinity. None of the Africans and only two percent of the black American respondents indicated "each to his own." These data also reflected the black students' Afrocentric view of black relations.

Of the respondents who felt that black Americans should

be identified with Africa, one black American and 94 percent
of the Africans said it was because Africa is the black Americans' "ancestral origin." However, nine black Americans and
one black African respondent felt black Americans' identity
with Africa and Africans is based upon "cultural roots." Fifteen percent of the black Americans felt black Americans'
identity with Africa occurs because both have "common aspirations and goals," that is, trying to free themselves from their
common oppressor. However, none of the African respondents
saw this to be the case. Nine black Americans felt the need for
identification with Africa and Africans because both groups
"need each other" in their common struggles. Here, too, only
one African respondent said this was the case.

It is interesting to note that most African respondents see
that the common bonds that unite them to black Americans
are based upon "ancestry and color."

One thing that these data clearly present is the fact that both
groups of respondents have an Afrocentric view. They feel a
strong bond for black Americans to be identified with Africa
and Africans. The Africans' overwhelming choice of "ancestry"
points this out. Common ancestry is one of the strongest bonds
of mankind. The Africans' acceptance of their black American
brothers and sisters indicates this close and warm affinity. The
black Americans' concern with identification with Africa and
Africans and their choices of external attributes point to their
discomfort, restlessness, and protest in knowing that there are
still some pockets of colonization and imperialism on African
soil. The Africans' plight of oppression and suppression by alien
powers makes them feel these common bonds, bonds based upon
a people having to suffer on their own soil as those in far-away
places. Black American respondents who chose to be identified
with America gave reasons concerning their need to fight here
in America in an effort to make America a safer and better
place for black people and other peoples of color.

When the list of reasons given for black Americans' identification with Africa are analyzed, according to the dimensions of
identity (internal/external), interesting patterns emerge. Africans
eight to one, chose the internal dimensions of identity; black
Americans chose, eleven to one, the external dimensions of

identity. Most African respondents come from already politically independent states and perhaps consider the affinity based upon blood and flesh as the most important identity factor. However, black Americans see external conditions as the most pressing for them and other blacks around the world, including such aspects as political oppression and suppression by whites of people of color and common goals in terms of political, social, and economic freedom from white races.

Overwhelmingly, both groups of respondents chose "Black Africa" as the best and most viable place for black Americans to be identified with. This is in concert with other dimensions of identity dealt with so far. Blacks, in general, do like, admire, and identify with one another. These data indicate the closeness of the bonds the respondents feel.

Where Black American Students Wish to Move and Live

Another item that attests to the close affinity between black Americans and Africans is the answer given when black American respondents were asked whether they would live in Africa if an opportunity arose to do so. (See Table 3.) Here, 70 percent of the black American students said they would certainly move to Africa to live, while only 28 percent indicated that they would not. Here, too, though the data indicate that the majority of black-American students wish to live in Africa, a few feel that even if the opportunity arose, they would not wish to move to Africa to live. This information is in tune with that which dealt with black movements to Africa. It seems as if those who took an interest in such matters might have zeroed in on the few who expressed their need not to immigrate to Africa and concluded that most black Americans did not want to immigrate to Africa and hence did not like or identify themselves with Africans or Africa. Here, our interest lies with the majority of the respondents who have answered that they would like to live in Africa. The issue here is to deal with majority feelings, rather than generalizing from the minority point of view.

Those black American respondents who indicated that they

TABLE 3

Black Americans Who Would Live in an African Country

Responses	Black Americans	
	Number	Percentage
Yes	28	70
No	11	28
No Response	1	2
Total	40	100

would live in Africa if they had a chance to do so were asked to name their choice of countries to which they would like to immigrate.[2] Fifty-three percent of black American respondents chose East African countries, 27 percent chose Central and South African countries, and 13 percent said they did not know which countries they would like to move to.

Those who chose their favorite countries to which to immigrate if an opportunity arose were asked further to state the reasons why they chose those particular countries: "That is where we originated," "I have heard so much about it," "I can speak the native language," and "To help free Africans still under colonial rule" were some of the responses. The respondents' selection of eastern African countries and certain west African countries might have been influenced by the fact that there was heavy representation among the African students and members of the faculty from both East and West African countries—particularly from Kenya, Ethiopia, Tanzania, Nigeria, and Ghana. Most of the respondents gave varied reasons for choosing their favorite countries. Two salient reasons for choosing their favorite countries were: "because I have heard so much about it" and because of the "favorable climatic conditions" attributed particularly to eastern African countries, such as Kenya and Zimbabwe and South Africa. Kenya and Ethiopia were favorably remembered from the results of international sports events at the Olympic games in Mexico. Other respondents indicated that they were interested in living in the countries of their choice because they spoke the language, referring to the Kiswahili language, which was being offered at institutions where the respondents studied.

However, the respondents who had chosen some of the western parts of the African continent seemed to have done so because of the influence of history. Many of them indicated that they had learned that most of the slaves who were transported to America and elsewhere originated predominantly from these West African countries. Most of the respondents felt that if ever they had a homeland to return to, it must be somewhere along the western coast of Africa.

Others chose countries like Ethiopia, Ghana (Ashanti), and Kenya (Mau Mau) because of these countries' resistance to foreign domination, which the respondents seemed greatly to admire—particularly for violent opposition to colonial regimes. One respondent chose Algeria "due to the fact that as it stands now it is the *only* country I know that will accept us as brothers and sisters." The Ashantis are admired for their warlike resistance and for their art and culture, which date back several centuries. Ethiopia is admired because it was one of the oldest states in the entire continent of black Africa with African traditional rulers. In addition, Nigerians are respected for their art and history and the sympathetic feelings that came from the wide coverage of the Nigerian civil war. As one of the respondents said, "they are places I hear most talked about, and maybe I would do something to help the starving Biafrans." The horrors shown by the starving Nigerian children left deep impressions that the respondents seemed unable to forget. Some respondents chose South Africa because they wanted to free the South Africans from their political oppression and suppressive conditions. "Because of the degree of racism I would like to institute a movement to rid this part of Africa from total White domination," one respondent added. The plight of black South Africans is well known among black Americans. They identify themselves with still-colonized white-ruled South Africa. Most black American respondents want all the black African nations to be free because that would help blacks wherever they may be. One respondent said: "One which is governed by blacks with the theme of a United Black World and concrete methods of nationalism leaning towards this; this is what I believe in." Africa is important to black Americans not only as a place to which they might move, but also because of special emotional ties through genealogical identity, cultural and historical similarities, and many other aspects of black life in the United States.

Some of the respondents had met African students who told them about their countries, while others had relatives or friends who had been to Africa. On this, one respondent said "just because I had the experience of conversing with a black American and his reaction to this country wasn't favorable" (Ethiopia). Other young people were able to go to Africa through various youth exchange programs, such as the United States Government's Peace Corps and the privately sponsored Cross-Roads Africa, and with various religious and civic organizations. But none of the present respondents indicated that they had been to Africa. Most of their information about Africa was obtained by reading, by meeting Africans, and from movies, television, and other secondary sources. One respondent said: "I have seen pictures of the events, schools and the people who look most friendly." Another added: "If I had to [I'd get to] the most modern [country] though (not so) modern part of Africa."

However, after talking to the black American respondents, almost all of them expressed the need to go to Africa, at least for a visit. Many of them also indicated that they plan to go to Africa someday. Since these were students, they were asked where they would go if they had a chance to study abroad. A list of five continents from which to choose was provided for the respondents. (See Table 4.) The data showed that an overwhelming majority of American respondents said they would definitely go to an African university to study (90 percent). Only 7.5 percent of the respondents chose Latin American and Australian universities.

Here, too, black American respondents seemed more inclined to go to Africa to study than to any other continent. They like the prospect and hope that someday they would find them-

TABLE 4

Black Americans Who Would Study Abroad

Choices	Black Americans	
	Number	Percentage
Africa	36	90.0
Europe	0	0.0
Latin America	3	7.5
Asia	0	0.0
Australia	1	2.5
Total	40	100.0

selves in Africa. This strong identification of black people for one another has been clearly demonstrated by what the respondents felt they had in common with one another; black Americans' identification with Africa, and the students' choice to go to Africa for future studies if opportunities arose. The second step was to try to find out if black peoples' identification with one another was perceived to be only along ancestral and racial identities. If it were so, one might be led to argue that this obvious argument did not really tell us much, as everybody knows that these two groups of blacks are related in terms of those dimensions.

Things They Liked and Admired Most about One Another

In order to find out from the students' personal and informal lives what projected selves the respondents saw in each other, both groups were asked to state: "What are some of the things that you like and admire most about black Africans?" Black Americans admired and liked black Africans; they said that Africans are "dignified, beautiful people in their culture and customs."[3] This point is very important, because it has long been held that black Americans have always been ashamed of their blackness and thus their association with Africans and Africa from longstanding myths and stereotypes had been developed and perpetuated in order to degrade black people.

Since it is believed that black Americans' image of Africa is that of shame and self-denigration based on myths and stereotypes, I thought it important to probe deeper in a round-about way. The respondents from both groups were asked, "What are some of the things that you like and admire most about Black-Americans/Africans?" First, we shall look at what black American respondents said they liked and admired most about their black African counterparts.

Things That Black Americans Liked and Admired Most about Black Africans

INTERNAL DIMENSIONS OF IDENTITY

"The fact that we are all Africans."

"That black Americans can identify with black Africans."

"Intelligence, beauty in themselves and their country."

"Black Africans are proud, strong, intelligent, and fun-loving."

"They are my brothers and sisters."

"Basically all since we are the same people."

EXTERNAL DIMENSIONS OF IDENTITY

Black Pride and Awareness

"Their pride in their heritage."

"Their black-awareness."

"Speech and pride in self."

"Their awareness."

"The majority of black Africans that I have met are very aware and *very* real."

"I like the way they carry themselves."

"Their pride, and mannerisms, knowledge of their heritage, and language. Unity and love for themselves."

"They give information which I feel is valuable to my knowledge of the high culture black people have had long before the white man ever came from all four winds."

"Culture, arts, and contributions towards awareness."

Personality, Behavior, and Mannerisms

"Honest to the point, willing to adapt to change."

"Pleasant personality."

"They are friendly and very warm people."

"Friendliness, and cooperative ways."

"Honesty, easy to talk to, greetings."

"Pleasant personality, politeness."

"They are very friendly, like to party, and to socialize."

"Don't know them very well; the ones I know are very nice people."

"Willing to adapt to change, language, speech."

"The majority's ability to express themselves."

"Their native tongue."

As a matter of fact, in one way or another, most black Americans mention black Africans' intellectual ability more than any other aspect named. This fact should be stressed, since racists have believed that black people, in general, are of lower intelligence than other races. Blacks in this study did not hold this belief. The data indicated that black Americans do like and admire black Africans and that they consider black Africans "beautiful people." There is literature showing that the self-image of black Americans changed considerably after seeing black African heads of state at the United Nations and the White House. The independence of black African nations has also helped Afro-Americans view themselves more positively as blacks.[4] What emerges is a healthy and wholesome positive self-identification among black American respondents. Other issues that were discussed pointed to deeper issues such as "honesty" and "warmth."

Now let us consider what black Africans like and admire most about their black American counterparts. Black Africans were asked to state what they liked and admired most about their black American brothers and sisters.

Things Black Africans Liked and Admired Most about Black Americans

INTERNAL DIMENSIONS OF IDENTITY

"Feeling black."

"Courageous, aware and proud of their being black—not as brainwashed as we Africans are."

"The desire to be black and proud."

"Racial pride and grand consciousness."

"Search for identity."

"Black pride."

EXTERNAL DIMENSIONS OF IDENTITY

Personality, Behavior, and Mannerisms

"Courage to express themselves."

"They say it like it is."

"Honesty, openness, sociability."

"Simplicity of their manner and the easy way in which they socialize."

"Loving, strong, intelligent, human, with faults, concerned about brothers."

"Outspoken, sincere, and interested in social problems."

"Patience, compassionate."

"Directness, openness."

"Friendliness and cheerfulness."

Gifts and Talents

"Dance, music, carefree, and sports."

"Exercise of talents, for example, in music."

"Music, dance, athletic ability."

"Energetic, especially in music, dance, and athletic superiority."

Oppression/Suppression

"The struggle against oppression and racism in America, the honesty and open-mindedness in some of them."

"Fight for freedom and a sense of dignity."

"They are hardworking, they seem to know what they are doing and why they are there in the United States—their strife for independence."

"Cooperative against white racism."

"A fantastic sense of self-determination."

"Getting rid of white oppression."

BLACK PRIDE AND AWARENESS

The second most salient attribute that black Americans liked and admired about their black African counterparts had to do with the Africans' pride in themselves, their culture and nations, and with the proud way Africans carry themselves. African heritage is embodied in these few young Africans in the United States. To me, this is a crucial point since Eurocentrists believe that blacks in general are ashamed of their culture and ethnic heritage; this category was overwhelmingly mentioned by most respondents in this study. If there is shame in blackness no evidence in these data suggests it.

When we move into the cultural area, we find that black American respondents do like and admire the African culture and heritage. This African culture is manifested through the

Africans' "colorful dress," "politeness," "pride in themselves," their "versatility in many languages," and "their friendliness." African cultural essence can be seen everywhere in the Africans' own being.

Some black African respondents said they admired their black American brothers and sisters' sense of "black pride." Black pride involves, among other things, color as well as cultural pride. If black Africans did not like these and identified themselves with black Americans, then it should have been assumed that black Africans do not like nor identify themselves with their black American counterparts. Yet, black pride is the first attribute that black Africans named. Black Africans were extremely impressed by some black Americans' sense of nationalism. One of the African respondents said, "Some of them are so African, more so than I am." Black Americans' wearing of the African mode of dress, Afro hairdos, and changing their names to African names were other indications of a sense of nationalism. The Americans' fervent quest for things African has given the Africans a sense of pride in themselves and other blacks in general. They tended to find the black Americans' sense of identification with Africa and Africans extremely impressive, as one African indicated when he said, "In order to see a real African, I guess one has to come to the United States to find him. In Africa, we are still struggling to become as Western as we can possibly be, but here they are trying to be as African as they can possibly be."

Africans have not failed to notice some black Americans' practices that they see as being "very African" concerning things African. Black Americans are seen as being very open and genuine in their dealings with other people. "They speak their minds openly, what they feel and how they feel about certain people. They do not hesitate nor try to salvage anything. They have open minds and a fantastic sense of honesty." They often speak out without fear of anybody or anything. This is extremely impressive to black Africans.

Equally significant was the black Americans' sense of "rhythm, music, dance"—their general sense of carrying themselves proudly and their sense of balance and rhythm. Africans are very much aware of black Americans' contributions in these cultural areas. Black Americans set the tone and pace of these activities for American society and, subsequently, for the world.

Athletic ability also was seen as one of the strongest contributions of black Americans—particularly as some sports in America are dominated by black Americans. Africans remember most vividly the black Americans' splendid showing at the Olympic games, which brings a fantastic sense of pride to Africans and other black people. The superior physical performances of black Americans is a matter of indisputable record.

On another plane, the Africans see black Americans' "sense of determination to survive in a dominantly hostile society" as a special gift to be greatly admired. Most of these Africans have come from recently independent nations. They know and understand oppression and suppression. The fact that black Americans have endured such conditions for so long against overwhelming odds amazes Africans.

Some answers listed under "other" were indicative of those deeper admired qualities, such as "their struggle against oppression and racism in America." One respondent said, "A fight for freedom and a sense of dignity," and other added, "their struggle for independence." Still another mentioned "their cooperation against racism" and "search for self-determination, getting rid of oppression."

Besides all these, some respondents reflected a further and deeper understanding of their black sisters and brothers' deeper qualities that could only come from close observation. These ranged all the way from "honesty and openmindedness" to: "Black Americans are hard-working and seem to know what they are doing in the United States." Another respondent spoke of "courage, friendliness, cheerfulness, and their interest in trying to solve social problems." "They are very sincere, energetic, patient, and compassionate people." There are other things such as "simplicity of manner and the easy way they socialize," one respondent concluded.

Black Americans' African Survivals

Most black African students felt that they could easily detect and identify social strands that they felt were quite African,

for example, the black Americans' generosity. One African
respondent explained it this way:

> A black American is the only one who would want to
> offer and share with you what he has, even if it means that
> it is the very last one he has. He would ask you, for ex-
> ample, if you wanted a bite or a sip. They are the only
> ones I know of who do so. Now I have seen the same
> thing copied by whites, particularly hippies. He will drink
> from the same cup, can, or straw. They are just like us
> black Africans. This could never happen with members
> of any other groups that I know of. Even if it does, the
> other groups that I know will try and find you another
> glass to offer you some of his drink. Or even further still,
> he might buy you another hamburger instead of sharing
> his with you. Or he might bring you another plate, but
> hardly the same container.

Another respondent added:

> When you meet a black anywhere, just anywhere, even if
> you do not know him and he you, he will greet you. Even
> if he does not know you, even if he does not, he will at
> least give you a glance or just a nod to show you that he
> has seen you, he recognizes you. You exist for him and
> he for you. It is such a wonderful thing. I love it. These
> people are, indeed, Africans!

Another respondent, who had been in the United States during the racial riots in the 1960s, remembered that blacks set
fires, broke windows, and looted all over his neighborhood,
but when they came to where he and other black African students lived, they stopped destroying the property because they
found out that black Africans and brothers were living there,
rather than whites. He had very vivid impressions of this event
as he related it:

> I was so impressed and so thankful that I was black,
> since then, I have come to love and respect them. I am

not afraid of them as I was told to be by my white
friends. I am all the way for and with them. Their fate
and mine is closely linked as black people. There is no
way one can really and truly escape the simple fact. I feel
protected and secure here [this respondent lived in the
ghetto]. I know they would not hurt me if they knew
that I am with them all the way. They are my people,
and I am one of them. America has been unfair to them
and I think they deserve everything that America can
offer to others. After all, they also made America what
it is today—a truly great nation. If I were to be asked
where I stand, I'd have to stand right beside them and be
counted. There are no two ways about it.

In general, black Africans do feel very close affinity with
their black American brothers and sisters. They are sensitive
to the immense injustices that have been done to them and
recognize their inner good qualities about which other Americans do not seem so sensitive. These inner qualities and understanding can only come from those who have been quite close
to their counterparts and understand them as human beings
who are and have been long misunderstood, mistreated, and
for the most part, ignored. Thus, black Africans are not in-
sensitive to the plight of their black American brothers and
sisters.

Throughout this chapter we have learned several things.
First, it is true that black Americans and Africans share an
identity based upon their common ancestry and hence color.
But more important, it has been revealed that they share a
common identity through the external dimensions of identity,
such things as common social-cultural heritage, oppression
and suppression. Second, black American respondents expressed
a willingness to immigrate to Africa if opportunities arose. What
should be noted and stressed here is the fact that there was a
minority group who chose to remain within the United States,
28 percent, as opposed to 70 percent of the respondents
who clearly expressed the need to move to Africa to live. However, an examination into some reasons given by black American respondents who chose to remain in the United States

instead of moving to any of the other five continents, reveals an important aspect probably never examined closely before. They wanted to remain in the United States "to fight here and try to make United States a better place for blacks and other minorities." They stayed here for positive rather than negative reasons. Third, the respondents from both groups seemed to like and admire their counterparts on the basis of ancestry, color, and, above all, other attributes not commonly credited to blacks as a people. Fourth, the Africans commented on several things about black Americans, as indicated by the few illustrations given, that they feel are "very African" indeed.

Notes

1. Robert D. Cohen, "African Students and the Negro-American Past Relationships and Recent Programs," *International and Cultural Exchange* 5 (Fall 1969): 76-85.

2. Number of cases = 30.

3. These are some of the salient characteristics named by the respondents.

4. Harold Isaacs, *The New World Negro Americans* (New York: Compass Books Edition, 1964), pp. 105-322 gives an excellent treatment of attitudes toward Africa before the independence of many nations there.

5.
Black American and African Patterns of Social Interaction

The review of the literature on black American and African social relations given in Chapter 1 pointed to three findings: First, black Americans and Africans do not, in general, interact with each other socially. Second, whatever social interactions exist, more often than not, are viewed as strained. Third, a reason given for this lack of relationship and the presence of strain is "cultural difference."

In this chapter we look at several factors that could give us insight into black relationships. First we examine each respondent's friends, asking their nationality, race, sex, and occupation and under what circumstances they met. Second, we zero in on what both groups perceive to be the nature and extent of the social interactions between them.

As it is believed that black Americans and Africans do not generally interact socially, respondents from both groups were asked to name three of their best friends, excluding both close and distant relatives. For each friend, the respondents were asked to indicate how they met and to give their friends' occupation, race, nationality, and sex.

Table 5 shows the findings on nationality. Data on friends' nationality showed that 55 percent of the black American respondents had other "Americans" as their three best friends, while 30 percent of the Africans had other "Africans" as their best friends. However, 7.5 percent of black American respondents indicated that their three best friends were all Africans.

TABLE 5

Closest Friends' Nationality

Responses	Black Americans		Black Africans		Total	
	Number	Percentage	Number	Percentage	Number	Percentage
Americans	22	55.0	2	5.0	24	30.0
Africans	3	7.5	12	30.0	15	18.8
Some Americans and some Africans	12	30.0	14	35.0	26	32.6
Other	0	0.0	11	27.5	11	13.6
No Response	3	7.5	1	2.5	4	5.0
Total	40	100.0	40	100.0	80	100.0

On this issue only 5 percent of the Africans indicated that their three best friends were all Americans.

On the other hand, 30 and 35 percent of the black American and African respondents indicated that their three best friends came from assorted nationalities, that is, "Americans and Africans."

Also, 27.5 percent of the black Africans indicated that they had members of other nationalities, besides Africans and Americans, as their best friends. This group of best friends might be members of other nationalities that the African students have managed to meet through their various international organizations in many campuses. They, as foreign students rather than black American students, are more likely to meet other foreign students from many lands. Most of these foreign student organizations form a mini-United Nations on many American campuses, where the foreign students meet and work. Respondents were asked to identify the racial groups of their three best friends. (See Table 6.)

Here data indicated that 90 percent of the black American respondents' best friends were from the "black" racial group, while 27.5 percent of the black Africans indicated that all their best friends were "black."

No black Americans indicated that all three of their best friends were "white," while on this issue a substantial number of black Africans indicated that their three best friends all were "white" (38 percent).

Also, only 7.5 percent of the black Americans and 27.5 percent of the black Africans indicated that their three best friends were of "assorted" racial groups, both black and white.

Five percent of the black Africans indicated that their best friends were from "other" racial groups, other than blacks or whites, while none of the black American respondents indicated this case.

Here, too, the data suggested that black Africans, more than black Americans, tend to choose their best friends from racial groups other than that of their own. Perhaps this indicates that the choice of best friends was made in terms of the particular individuals rather than along racial lines and color per se.

TABLE 6

Closest Friends' Racial Group

Choices	Black Americans Number	Black Americans Percentage	Black Africans Number	Black Africans Percentage	Total Number	Total Percentage
All Black	36	90.0	11	27.5	47	58.7
All White	0	0.0	15	38.0	15	18.8
Black and White	3	7.5	11	27.5	14	17.5
Other	0	0.0	2	5.0	2	2.5
No Response	1	2.5	1	2.0	2	2.5
Total	40	100.0	40	100.0	80	100.0

This point was also noted in the University of California at Los Angeles study as the author states:

> It is striking that in the entire gamut of responses, including the most critical ones, the racial factor was either ignored or viewed as irrelevant in inhibiting friendship with whites. The many criticisms voiced were of American shallowness and lack of sincerity. Such comments are indistinguishable from those of other foreign students, including Europeans and Canadians, as was noted by many previous investigators.[1]

This point will be dealt with later, in more detail. It will suffice to mention here that the UCLA study has revealed another dimension about the foreign students in this country, that their overall reaction to Americans is that they display shallowness in their friendship patterns and a lack of sincerity. This might be true also concerning the Africans, when they view the black Americans just as any other Americans, without taking into consideration their special relationships based on color as well as genealogy. Also, as Africans, more than black Americans, seem to have friends from all racial groups and as their relationships seem smooth, they might tend to think that race has nothing to do with determining the various friendship patterns that they might enter. The Africans who indicated that their three best friends are all white amounted to 38 percent of the sample. This percentage is higher than for Africans relating to other Africans only.

There is a tendency on the part of the black African to assess all Americans in terms of their individual unique characteristics. It is not that all black Americans see their world in terms of color and that all Africans tend to see theirs as colorless, but this factor can be viewed in terms of its historical background. In most parts of Africa, Africans, though subjected to colonialism and a color bar, are always in the majority. Most African students have been to other European countries where racial discrimination is not as great as in the United States. When Africans are discriminated against racially for the first time in America, they cannot believe that people's skin color would matter so much as to deny them a decent job, house, education, or any other amenity the rest of the population enjoys. As most African students belong to international groups on campus that cater to foreign students from all over the world, they tend to forget differences in race, nationality, religion, and ethnicity.

This issue might indicate that black Americans, still suppressed and oppressed, might not want to interact socially with members of the oppressive/suppressive class, the whites. White Americans who are generally warm, kind, and hospitable to foreign students do not generally extend the same hospitality to their black American counterparts. White Americans' eagerness to be hospitable to foreign students brings about conflicting situations that affect African students' loyalty to either group of Americans. This issue will be discussed later when dealing with social strains between black Americans and Africans.

Another question concerning the respondents' racial friendship networks is: Why do most black American respondents recruit almost all of their best friends from their own racial group, more than black Africans? It is believed that this is due to different social, economic, political, and cultural backgrounds that are predominantly American in nature. Differences could be due to the higher social-class background of some African respondents in this study. They are the elites, and thus they associate with whites.

It is significant that black Africans come from backgrounds where a traditional African way of life predominates and where Africans were and are in the majority for the most part. On the whole, most black Africans, except in places like South Africa, have been less affected by racial discrimination than black Americans. First, black Africans have been in the majority in most situations, while black Americans remain in social situations where they have been and still are considered as a minority. Second, in many African countries, colonialism lasted less than a hundred years. And third, Africans have remained in their homelands following a traditional way of life and have not been forcibly torn away and transported to alien lands as

were the ancestors of black Americans. Most whites living in
Africa, even those with a colonial mentality, have adjusted their
attitudes towards blacks either as a result of genuine concern
or economic need in order to survive in Africa in the future.
In addition, black Africans have always had the choice of returning to rural areas where the African way of life predominates if the constraints of an alien urban way of life become too
difficult.

A lesson to be learned from these data is that, contrary to
common belief, black people do not hate white people for
their color. Time and again, fingers are pointed at some violent
overthrow of white imperialists or the expulsion of the yellow
race from some countries. People are quick to say, "See, it is a
racial issue." What is often forgotten is the fact that black
people and others do not hate or dislike people because of the
color of their skin. They hate and dislike suppressive and oppressive political, social, economic, and cultural structures set up by
these people, who also happen to be predominantly white.
What these data show is that once these oppressive and suppressive structures are removed then people of diverse racial
backgrounds can find reasons based upon their other human
attributes and qualities either to qualify or to eliminate them
as friends. Genuine friendship cannot be forged under social
situations based on inequalities, but genuine friendship can be
established and thrive in a social climate of equality.

Hence whites' fears that if blacks are liberated they are going
to revenge those atrocities that whites have inflicted upon them
for centuries is unfounded. Historical experiences have indicated
otherwise. Witness many new African nations; none of them
since gaining political independence has said to their former
white overlords to ship out because they are white; Instead,
they have given them the opportunity either to accept the nonwhite leadership or to leave.

The fact that the respondents from both groups chose
members of their own race as their best friends also indicates
they felt common identity and affinity to one another. (See
Table 7.)

Concerning the sex of their best friends, an overwhelming

TABLE 7

Closest Friends' Sex

Responses	Black Americans		Black Africans		Total	
	Number	Percentage	Number	Percentage	Number	Percentage
All Same Sex	1	2.5	9	22.5	10	12.5
All Opposite	1	2.5	5	12.5	6	7.5
Both Sexes	35	87.5	20	50.0	55	68.8
No Response	3	7.5	6	15.0	9	11.2
Total	40	100.0	40	100.0	80	100.0

majority of the respondents, both black Americans and Africans, indicated they recruited their best friends from members of both sexes.

The slightly higher percentages of African respondents having all their best friends of their own sex can be attributed to the fact that there are more African males than African females on the campuses. From data on occupational status, it appears that many of these friends tend to be other male graduate students and colleagues from work, as well as people from their own countries. Also, data indicate the sex ratio among the black American respondents was one to one, while black African males were over-represented.

When the respondents' friends' occupations are closely examined, data indicate that most of the respondents seem to have friends from the same occupational status (student) as themselves. However, some respondents did name friends from a much higher occupational status, such as teachers and supervisors. Some 12.5 percent of black Americans and 25 percent of Africans indicated they had networks of social interaction across different occupations.

On the other hand, a significantly lower percentage of the respondents indicated that some of their friends were from a lower occupational status. This is also expected, since at most institutions of higher learning or otherwise, the occupational status of a student is one of the lowest in the college or university's occupational rank and file. (See Table 8.)

However, the black Americans, more than the Africans, tended to have friends of assorted occupational ranks, from "lower," "middle," and "higher" occupational status. Thirty-two and a half percent of black American and 57.5 percent of African respondents indicated that their best friends were of either "equal" occupational status or "lower" than themselves.

Over a half of black African respondents indicated that their best friends have the "same" occupational status as themselves, indicating that many of them show occupationally endogamous friendship networks among themselves. Half as many black Africans as black Americans claimed friends in higher occupational echelons, which could be attributed to their much easier

TABLE 8

Closest Friends' Occupational Status

Compared to Respondent	Black Americans		Black Africans		Total	
	Number	Percentage	Number	Percentage	Number	Percentage
Same as	12	30.0	21	52.5	33	41.0
Higher than	5	12.5	10	25.0	15	19.0
Lower than	1	2.5	2	5.0	3	4.0
Assorted Occupational Status	22	55.0	7	17.5	29	36.0
Total	40	100.0	40	100.0	80	100.0

employability in occupations with a higher than student status.
This gave them a slight advantage in having members of higher
occupational echelons as colleagues. Also, members of the
higher occupational status groups often adopt foreign students,
becoming their American foster parents. Many foreign students
in America also have a chance to address various international,
national, and local groups, where they meet the local occupational elite.

Although most of the respondents are quite young, and this
generational group is thought in most instances to be anti-
materialism, anti-status quo and anti-system, these data indicate that their sympathies do not necessarily lie with the underdogs; rather, they seem to have close friends who are of the
same or higher social status than themselves.

Black American and African Perceptions
of Their Social Interactions

A key issue often used as an indicator that black Americans
and Africans do not, in general, identify with one another is
the lack of social interaction between them. It was deemed
essential to find out what the respondents from both groups
perceived to be the nature and extent of their own social interactions. The subjects from both groups were asked "To what
extent would you say that Black-Americans and Africans interact socially?" (See Table 9.)

The data indicated that 88 percent of black American respondents felt that black Americans and Africans "sometimes" interacted socially. Seven percent of them felt that social interactions
between black Americans and Africans took place "often,"
while a very small percentage, 5 percent, felt that social interactions took place "always."

Seventy-three percent of the African respondents felt that
black Americans and Africans interact "sometimes," 25 percent
said black social interactions take place "often," and a very
small percentage, 2 percent, said that black social interactions
took place "always."

TABLE 9

Extent to Which Black Americans and Africans Interact Socially

| Responses | Black Americans | | Black Africans | |
	Number	Percentage	Number	Percentage
Never interact socially	0	0	0	0
Sometimes interact socially	35	88	29	73
Often interact socially	3	7	10	25
Always interact socially	2	5	1	2
Total	40	100	40	100

This point is significant, as the examination of the Eurocentric view (see Chapter 1) indicated that relationships between black Americans and Africans are almost nonexistent and that whatever relationships do exist are often characterized as strained. These data indicate not only that relationships between black Americans and Africans exist but that they are seen as very strong. The strength of the relationships is indicated by all respondents; both black Americans and Africans say that relationships between them do exist. As all the respondents said that social interactions do exist between the groups, one is led to believe that the respondents also interacted socially with members of the other group.[2]

The next question is: What are the respondents' perceptions as to the nature and extent of their own black social interactions? Here, the respondents from both groups were asked to state the nature of the relationships between black Americans and Africans. Black social interactions data indicate there are no significant nationality differences when it comes to what the respondents felt about their mutual social interactions. (See Table 10.)

It is significant to note here that 10 and 13 percent of the black American and African respondents respectively indicated that they perceived their social interactions to be free of social strains. However, the overwhelming perceptions among respon-

TABLE 10

The Nature of Black American and African Social Interactions

Responses	Black Americans		Black Africans	
	Number	Percentage	Number	Percentage
Social interactions are never strained	4	10	5	13
Social interactions are occasionally/sometimes strained	32	80	28	70
Social interactions are always strained	4	10	7	17
Total	40	100	40	100

dents from both groups is that their social interactions were "occasionally strained," with the total of 80 percent of black American respondents and 70 percent of African respondents feeling that way. Only a very small percentage within each group of the respondents, 10 percent black Americans and 17 percent Africans who socially interact with one another managed to find their social interactions "always strained."

The next question was what the subjects perceived to be the causes of their strained relationships. A large number from both groups indicated that their relationships were strained because of external dimensions, such as oppression, suppression, cultural differences, and the like. None of the respondents felt that strained relationships were a result of internal dimensions of identity, that is, "color or ancestry." This is important because it is often believed that black people hate themselves because they are black! If this were true, then the respondents might have given some reasons pertaining to color or ancestry, but none of these respondents did. They all said that their strained relationships are caused by external dimensions of identity. (See Table 11.)

TABLE 11

Nationality and Dimensions of Felt Social Strains

Responses	Black Americans		Black Africans	
	Number	Percentage	Number	Percentage
Inapplicable (no strains)	4	10	5	13
Internal attributes (color/ancestry)	0	0	0	0
External attributes (oppression/suppression/ cultural/social)	36	90	35	87
Total	40	100	40	100

If we examine black American and African social strains within the context of either internal or external dimensions of identity, we note that of all the respondents from both groups who perceived a certain degree of strain within the relationship, 100 percent of them perceived social strains as having their roots within external dimensional sources and having nothing at all to do with internal dimensions.

But before we move on, let us break down some of the important salient features mentioned most often under the external dimension of identity as causing strain.

African Social Interactions with Whites

The data show that 33 percent of black American respondents indicated that their social relationships were often marred because of the Africans' "social interactions with whites." This reason was at the top of the list of attributes mentioned. That black Americans and not Africans would consider black peoples' social interactions with whites as cause for strain could be explained by the fact that, as black unity is so essential to black people, there might be a feeling that blacks should not hold close relationships with those defined as the enemy. In general, white Americans tolerate the presence of Africans in this country, knowing that they will eventually return to their countries of origin once their studies are completed. Africans, unlike black Americans, do not constitute an economic threat as do their black American counterparts. The role played by an African in this country is that of a "stranger" who can move from one group to another by virtue of the "stranger" role with more relative ease than would be possible for either of the two native groups.

Black Americans who have indicated this about black Africans have added: "They, Africans, don't want to bother with us." Or, "If whites are around, for instance, or if the African somehow has been brainwashed." A third remarked: "Because I see what they do and not what they say." A fourth indicated: "They socialize with whites."

Black Americans' Ignorance about Africa and Africans

Another divergent perception concerning both groups was that black Africans overwhelmingly felt that their relationships with black Americans were marred because of black Americans' "ignorance concerning Africans and Africa." About half of the African respondents were of this opinion. This category claimed by far the largest response within this group. The black Americans did not indicate that a reason for black social strains was Africans' ignorance concerning black Americans.

The Africans perceived gross ignorance on the part of black Americans, including cultural ignorance that contributes to communication difficulties between the two parties concerned. The lack of knowledge on the part of black people about each other's true selves and the realities of their countries and cultures has proved to be a strain-causing factor. The Africans felt "stupid," and "foolish" questions were asked about them and their countries, "just as those the white people would ask" the Africans about their countries, cultures, and peoples. For instance, they asked if the Africans still "live in jungles, still eat human flesh, have a tail as a vestigial remain from evolutionary development, if they still walk around naked, if they live in huts." Such questions angered most of the African respondents. Sometimes Africans lost patience and realized that perhaps some of these questions were really genuine and that black Americans wanted to know the information from Africans themselves rather than the myths they had been given by the "middlemen."

Among the characteristics that black Africans disliked about their black American counterparts, "ignorance about Africa and Africans" stood at the top of the list. It was followed very closely by "superiority complex" feelings among black Americans. As one African respondent indicated: "They, too, hold the very same stereotypes that white society has held since time immemorial about the 'primitive' and the 'dark continent' of the African and Africa as depicted by Tarzan movies." Though black African respondents mentioned some special efforts that they have made to relate, both formally and informally, the facts about their modern African independent nations and their peoples, it seemed as if sometimes even black Americans, like the whites, found it hard to believe in or conceive of modern Africa—its people, towns, cities, electricity, permanent homes, streets and motorized transport, and the elites and the important roles they play in direct political control of their new nations, from which most of these students have come.

Besides black Americans' perception of Africans' social interactions with whites and black Africans' perception of black Americans' "ignorance about Africa and Africans," the rest of the attributes were mentioned with equal frequency by both groups of blacks. A small number among both Africans and black Americans gave other reasons for strained black social relationships, such as "it depends on the individuals involved."

Cultural Differences

"Cultural differences" were mentioned by both black Americans and Africans as a strain-causing element in the relationships. One of the black American respondents said, ". . . many black Africans think differently just because of value differences." The second said, "because of different customs, most of them I note are between African males and black American females." Another added, "Although we are all blacks, their values differ, for example, food, music, dating habits, speech, and professional aspirations." Black Africans had this to say concerning cultural differences: "We have different basic social and cultural values." One African respondent said, "They (black Americans) are different, and they act different because of differences in cultural upbringing." Another added, "We are both from different cultural and social experiences." A fourth said, "Because of cultural differences, customs and practices differ markedly."

Most respondents from both groups were of the opinion that there were basic cultural differences between the groups. These cultural differences are perceived insofar as one culture (African) is predominantly non-Western, whereas the other (American) is predominantly Western. Within this cultural dimension of strains, some of the respondents from both groups indicated that they were often "afraid to offend" one another. This offense is mainly anchored within the social-cultural backgrounds that these groups felt they did not have in common and often resulted in what some respondents called "hang-ups." An African respondent remarked, "This is due to hang-ups of both parties, Africans and Afro-Americans. They both just have to learn that we actually have more in common than we realize." Another added, "It is difficult to generalize; it depends on who one meets; blame cannot be pinned on one particular group only." A black American female added, "There yet has to be a genuine attempt of both parties to interact positively, otherwise a whole lot of phoniness will continue to prevail. The blame should be placed on both groups and not one."

Along cultural dimensions of strains, the respondents looked
down on each other's "cultural refinement." African views of
black American mannerisms ranged all the way from being
"loud, boisterous show-offs, and sometimes rudeness based
on no substance at all." Black American respondents viewed
Africans as "cold, serious, reserved, and emotionally indifferent, up-tight, and generally trying to be as gentlemanly as
'whitey.' " Black Americans interpreted the Africans' behavior
as consisting of the same general ingredients as the white population's general "up-tightness" and "hang-ups," which should not
be true of any black people. They felt that Africans are putting
on a white man's front. For, after all, are not black Americans'
free emotional and physical expressions part and parcel of the
very same substance that they all inherited from their Mother
Country, Africa? Thus the Africans are seen as trying to cover
up that which is said to be truly and genuinely beautifully
African in exchange for the Western-type "hang-ups" and "up-
tightness."

Another point where the two groups parted company is in
their respective modes of dress. With both groups, the male's
mode of dress was under vehement attack. African males' con-
servative form of dress—Western-cut suits, white shirts, ties, and
jackets—were seen by black American respondents as one female put it: "They are both dull and unexciting." Most Africans
admit this fact very readily and, as a matter of fact, some of
them stated that they "would never get caught dead in some
of the black American males' attire," especially the gaudy male
jumpsuits, the wearing of hair attachments and hats, and the
long, huge colorful coats to give the "superfly" look. They felt
these clothes were too colorful for males to wear. Even when
the Africans wear hats, they feel hats should be removed when
entering buildings and in the presence of ladies. Both groups
referred to each other's mode of dress as: "They do not know
how to dress."

The data show that 25 percent of black American and 30
percent of African respondents stated that there was "nothing"
in particular they disliked about each other.

Superiority/Inferiority Complex

The black Americans disliked Africans because they thought that Africans considered themselves superior to black Americans. However, when black Africans were asked if they felt superior to their black American counterparts, the Africans vehemently denied that they did. Also, an equal number of black Africans said that they thought that black Americans felt superior to black Africans. Black Americans were asked if they, indeed, felt this to be so; they also denied that attitude. If the respondents from both groups do not think or feel superior to their counterparts, how do some black respondents get this idea? The answer can be found in their responses. One black American respondent had this to say:

> We black people have been *lied to by the white man*. He has told us of the *myths* of the primitive Africans and told us that we are more like him (civilized). What he was doing all along was to try and make us align with him at the expense of our people (Africans) and ourselves (black Americans). [emphasis added]

A black African respondent said:

> It is a case of *long isolation* from one another. When I first came here and had not met any black Americans, some of my white friends told me all about them, you know how lazy they are, unambitious, unreasonably violent. At the same time, they emphasized how different the Africans are, proud, hard-working, and interested in high and best education. You know, I believed them then. It was not until much later that I came to realize *the distortion of facts* about racial discrimination and prejudice and their consequences. [emphasis added]

It is quite evident from the two responses that the groups do sense the reasons for their strained relationships—myths and stereotypes and the long process of isolation used to keep these two groups apart. In the center of it all, the culprit is the white man, who has acted as a middleman between the two groups. He first fabricated the myths and stereotypes as well as his successful attempt to keep these two groups isolated, one in forced bondage and the other in superimposed subjugation, and then he set himself up as a "broker." The message he carries to each is intended to benefit himself, not the two separated groups.

It is felt that this issue arose mainly from gross misunderstandings within both groups of blacks. For instance, it was discovered also during the course of this study that among the Africans who did not associate with black Americans, their reasoning was that black Americans felt that Africans associated with whites because Africans felt that they were better than their counterparts. However, some African students indicated that black Americans never invited them to their homes while whites did. Many Africans were apparently waiting for the black Americans to make the very important first step as hosts, since in Africa the host is the one who is to make the first step toward the guest and not the other way around. Africans indicated that they went only where they were invited and did not want to push themselves to social situations where they might not be wanted. Africans elaborated that white families and white institutions and organizations were always quick to do this; they did not see why black Americans should not do the same, rather than blaming them for associating with whites at the expense of blacks. Africans took this as a definite sign that their black American brothers and sisters do not want to have anything to do with Africans.

> Many of the Africans who came from the Mother continent have been *deceived* by the *whites* who *disillusions* them about their brothers and sisters. Many of them hardly visit the black community because of the *myths* they hold as told to them by the white people. [emphasis added]

Another black American added, ". . . because of the *lies* told
about one another by the *whites* through the mass media . . ."
[emphasis added].

Among the characteristics that black Africans disliked about
their black American counterparts, "ignorance about Africa and
Africans" stood at the top of the list. It was followed very closely by "superiority complex" feelings, which the Africans feel
Black-Americans hold toward Africans.

Some black Africans see black Americans as being generally
"unambitious," but this lack of ambition on the part of black
Americans, it is felt, should be placed within the context of
the American sociocultural background rather than being
viewed in isolation. The black American experience in a predominantly white racist society has for a long time denied them
of opportunities. It is even now true in some aspects of the
American social structural system that neither the black man's
education nor his money can buy him a place in the ranks of
humanity. It often does not matter how much education or
money the black man has: if he is black, then he is still considered black and remains an outsider. It seemed most Africans
found it hard to comprehend the fact that racial prejudice and
discrimination could be used to exclude a human being from
participating in the mainstream of American life. Some Africans
had to experience racial discrimination themselves before they
could realize that racial problems in America are real. They
realized finally that it was an American contradiction of terms
and practice. The so-called lazy and unambitious blacks did
help in building America as a nation, making the country one
of the strongest and richest nations in the world. The attributed
laziness came as a result of the deliberate exclusion of able-
bodied men and women from the fruits of their labors. What
appears as laziness may be a consequence of comparing the
kinds of African students that come to America—the high
achievers—to black students. Also, the definition of laziness
cannot be applied to the majority of black Americans if one
views the fact that the hard, dirty work in this country has been
done and is done by black Americans.

Among some "other" reasons given by Africans as attributes
they disliked about black Americans were such things as "dope."
Black Americans should certainly give up dangerous drugs that
are detrimental to the individual's health and the health of the
black community as a whole. They should use the money,
physical resources, and energies for the building and preservation of the black community in America. Africans see the drug
culture as definitely a defeatist and negative philosophy of life.
Instead, they feel they should apply their minds and money to
the welfare of their black communities. As one of the African
respondents indicated: "There is no way one is going to join
the revolution if one is perpetually under the influence of
drugs. These people are a disgrace to the black man's efforts to
free himself from suppression and oppression."

These data indicate that relationships between black Americans and Africans do indeed exist and are positive, contrary
to the view that whatever relationships existed were negative.
Both groups thought that social strains were generated by both
groups, whereas, as this study points out, these strains do not
come from black people but lie somewhere outside them with
the white groups who have come between black Americans and
Africans. They have come as a result of long-held myths fabricated to divide and conquer the blacks. The superiority/infer-
iority complex did not originate with blacks but was advanced
by whites in order to make it possible for the domination of
whites over blacks.

Cultural differences also come as a result of one culture being
defined as superior to another—the superior one being civilized
and Western, the other being defined by whites as inferior and
"primitive." The Africans' association with whites also caused
strained relationships between the two groups insofar as the
whites chose to associate with them and gave preferential treatment to the African blacks (strangers). Africans here for a
short time do not pose any economic threat to whites. Ignorance about Africa and things African also has to do with controls
the mass media has imposed upon the public—media that are
supposed to educate objectively the general public about the
Old World and the New.

Notes

1. U.S. Advisory Commission on International Educational and Cultural Affairs, *Foreign Students in the United States: A National Survey*, mimeographed (Washington, D.C., 1966), p. 14.

2. The category of black social interaction "never" taking place was also included in the initial choices given to the respondents but none of them, Africans or black Americans, indicated that social interactions between them "never" took place.

6

Perceived Proportions of Black American and African Social Interactions _____ with Whites

One burning issue that seems to divide the black American and African communities is that of Africans' social interactions with some members of the white community. The perceptions held by respondents from both groups are examined here concerning what they perceived to be the nature and extent of relations between blacks and whites.

First, we shall look into what the respondents estimated to be the proportion of social interaction with whites of their own group. Second, we shall examine the estimated proportion of the other group's social interaction with whites, and third, we shall consider how many respondents themselves answered that they do or do not interact socially with whites.

Perceived Black/White Social Interactions

The respondents from both groups were asked to estimate what they perceived to be the proportions of their own group's and the other group's social interactions with whites. (See Table 12).

Data inquiring into the estimated proportions of black American social interactions with whites present interesting patterns. Both groups of respondents were asked: In your own opinion, what proportion of black Americans do socialize with whites? Among the black American respondents, 82 percent

TABLE 12

Estimated Proportions of Black American Social Interactions with Whites

Perceived Proportions of Black American's Social Interactions with Whites	Black Americans		Black Africans		Total	
	Number	Percentage	Number	Percentage	Number	Percentage
None of them	7	18	0	0	7	8.7
Some of them	28	70	13	33	41	51.3
Most of them	4	10	20	50	24	30.0
All of them	1	2	7	17	8	10.0
Total	40	100	40	100	80	100.0

perceived black Americans socially interacting with whites in one degree or another. On the same issue, all black Africans perceived black Americans interacting socially with whites. Less than 20 percent among black Americans perceived "none" of the black Americans to socially interact with whites.

It is interesting to note that all respondents indicated that there exist some social interactions between the American blacks and whites. However, 70 percent of the black American and 33 percent of the African respondents indicated that "some" black Americans interact socially with whites, while 10 percent of the black Americans and 50 percent of the Africans indicated that "most" black Americans interact socially with white Americans. However, 2 percent of black American and 17 percent of African respondents said "all" black Americans interact socially with whites in one way or another.

On the same issue of what both groups perceived to be the proportions of black Africans who socially interacted with whites, data indicated that both groups of blacks perceived black Africans as interacting socially with whites, including black African respondents who admitted this fact to be true. (See Table 13.)

With regard to Africans' social interactions with whites, black American and African respondents indicated that all black Africans socially interacted with the whites in one way or another.

Eighty-five percent of black American and 83 percent of African respondents indicated that "some" Africans do associate with whites. When the degree of social interactions was raised to "most of them," data indicate 15 percent of black American and 7 percent of African respondents were of the opinion that "most" Africans do associate with whites, while none of the black American and 10 percent of the African respondents perceived "all" black Africans to interact with whites socially.

It is interesting to compare the figures on the proportions of the respondents as they view themselves and as they view others with respect to interaction with whites. As indicated in Table 13, 100 percent of the black Americans who responded

TABLE 13

Estimated Proportions of Black African Social Interactions with Whites

Perceived Proportions of Africans' Social Interactions with Whites	Black Americans		Black Africans		Total	
	Number	Percentage	Number	Percentage	Number	Percentage
None of them*	0	0	0	0	0	0
Some of them	34	85	33	83	67	84
Most of them	6	15	3	7	9	11
All of them	0	0	4	10	4	5
Total	40	100	40	100	80	100

*The respondents agree and believe that members of both groups do, in fact, socialize with members of the white community in one way or another whether social interactions are and would be classified as 'intimate' or 'superficial,' i.e., the inevitable social situations.

to this question indicated that in their own opinion they perceived that black Africans do socially interact with whites to one degree or another. Also, 100 percent of the black Africans felt the same about themselves interacting with the whites socially.

On the other hand, 82 percent of black American and 100 percent of African respondents perceived black interactions with the members of the white community. However, when data for both groups are compared, very interesting patterns emerge.

None of the black American respondents indicated that "all" Africans interact socially with the members of the white community. Here, 100 percent of the Africans see themselves as interacting socially with whites to "some" degree. On the other hand, 85 percent of black Americans think that "some" Africans interact with whites. As the degree of perceived social interactions among Africans and whites increases to "most," 7 percent of the Africans view themselves as interacting with whites to that degree, while black Americans increase the estimated social interaction to 15 percent. Ten percent of Africans feel that "all" of them interact socially with whites, while none of the black Americans perceived that "all" Africans interact socially with whites.

The way black Americans define their relationships with whites as well as the way they perceive their social interactions to be defined by Africans indicate that a surprisingly high proportion of American blacks, 70 percent, are of the opinion that "some" American blacks socially interact with whites, while only 33 percent of the African respondents perceive American blacks as engaging in such interactions.

However, as the proportion goes higher in degree to "most," only 10 percent of black Americans perceive their group as interacting socially with whites, while half of the black Africans perceive that "most" black Americans engage in such relationships. However, only 2 percent of the black American respondents were of the opinion that "all" black Americans socially interacted with whites, while a small percentage, 17 percent, of African respondents thought that "all" black Americans do, in fact, interact socially with whites.

The data indicated a tendency for members of one group to exaggerate the proportion of the other group who socially interact with whites, while each group seems to underestimate the proportion of their own group they feel socially interacts with whites. Concerning themselves, members of both groups seem to admit a relatively large proportion of social interaction with whites.

It is noted that 82 percent of black American respondents feel that they socialize with whites to one degree or another, while on the same point, all Africans view themselves this way. There are no differences when the respondents speak about themselves and the personal relationships they hold with the white community. Overall, there were no significant differences in black American perceptions of Africans or African perceptions of black Americans.

Before we comment further on perceived black social interaction with whites, let us examine the individual respondents' social interactions with whites. After respondents estimated the proportion of social interactions that they thought went on between their own group and whites as well as between the other black group and whites, it was time to try to zero in on whether the respondents themselves did or did not socialize with whites. (See Table 14.)

Here also, the data indicated that 55 percent of black American respondents said they socialized with whites, whereas a very large majority of African respondents, 90 percent, said they socialized with whites.

These data also confirmed the general perception that most black Africans interact socially with members of the white American community. There is nothing to indicate that these social interactions are racially exclusive; rather, they are a matter of degree.

Compared to the perceptions of the proportions of their own group's and the others group's social interactions with whites, the individual respondents indicated a higher degree of social interaction going on between blacks and whites when speaking of their own experience. Though this is true, how-ever, Africans seem to be the only ones blamed for such rela-

TABLE 14

Respondents' Own Social Interactions with Whites

Responses	Black Americans		Black Africans		Total	
	Number	Percentage	Number	Percentage	Number	Percentage
Yes	22	55	36	90	58	73
No	18	45	4	10	22	27
Total	40	100	40	100	80	100

tionships. Why? First, the African population in any given area is relatively small compared to that of black Americans. Since those few African students seem to interact with whites socially this gives the impression that all Africans socialize with whites. Second, it is generally true that African students have "intimate relationships with the members of the white community. For example, some of them had white families as guardians and/or sponsors. Third, some white families and their social organizations did take the trouble and interest to invite foreign students, of course including black African students, to their homes and associations, particularly during special events. Finally, black Africans, more often than not, did date whites to a larger extent than black Americans.

However, the most overwhelming discrepancies are indicated when the respondents are asked to state whether or not they themselves interact socially with members of the white community. The black Africans seem to be quite consistent on this issue, where 90 percent indicated that they interact socially with whites, a figure quite close to previous groups' estimates. Only 55 percent of black American respondents admitted that they interact socially with members of the white community. Why do black Americans seem to deflate their social interaction with members of the white community? It could be because of pressure on the members of the black community to cut off any social interactions with their white counterparts except for the superficial and informal ones, as a result of black nationalism that has swept the black community throughout the nation. Even so, should one think that black Africans are less nationalistically oriented than their black American brothers and sisters?

It can only be suggested here that Africans probably do not feel the same amount of pressure completely to sever ties already established with whites. Also, as already indicated, Africans have a tendency to try to associate with people according to the personalities of those concerned, rather than to reject whites as a group. Third, Africans might tend to view all Americans as Americans first and, despite color, tend to meet them on their own terms and merits rather than according to a more segmentized view of various racial groups. Fourth, their propensity to associate with nonblack foreign students from other foreign countries does greatly contribute to their higher degree of association with whites other than those from the United States. More importantly, few African students have really managed to enter and join black communities totally to enable them to view black Americans through black eyes.

Another point to be mentioned here is that blacks are so aware of offending social relationships among blacks and whites that they might see a few blacks who are viewed as "Uncle Toms" and might tend to exaggerate the degree of social relationships that are going on among blacks and whites.

Thus, in light of the data presented, this point does not seem to lend itself to easy and conclusive explanations, except that there may actually be more social interactions among black Americans and whites and among Africans and whites, however imposed or superficial, than blacks tend to admit. There may be some superficial relationships that appear at a distance to be informal and personal although they may not be so.

No viable socialization agencies have been given any formal functions of socializing these two groups, particularly the Africans. Most social encounters take place more or less on an ad hoc basis. There are no official channels of communication established to take care of intergroup communications. Empirical evidence from data dealing with Africans' stays in the United States indicates that the longer foreign students from any nation stay in the United States the more critical they become of the country and what goes on. Africans' negative reaction (in time) against the Western system, which is here equated with whites who control it, might give Africans reason to identify themselves with their black American brothers and sisters, insofar as they see themselves as black people who are, in this case, victims of the larger Western sociocultural system, which also happens to be predominantly white.

Another important factor is the fact that Africans know that they are going to live in the United States for a limited time. This might prompt them to consider their relationships with black Americans or with whites as temporary and hence lead to a lack of commitment to what they might consider as inherently internal problems that do not directly concern them. Identification or the lack of it does not necessarily stem from the fact that these are Africans from Africa, as opposed to black Americans in America, but rather from the contacts these groups have with each other.

From the data presented, several social strands emerge that seem to characterize the social relationships between blacks and whites. First, the majority of both black American and African respondents perceived that both black Americans and Africans interacted with whites socially, though 18 percent of black American respondents indicated that "none" of the black Americans socially interacted with whites. Second, when it came to perceiving black Africans' social interactions with whites, all respondents from both groups perceived all black Africans as socially interacting with whites. Third, only about half of black American and most black African respondents said they themselves socially interacted with whites. Fourth, black African respondents seemed to have more intimate social relationships with the members of the white community than their black American counterparts.

It is interesting to note, however, that though a relatively large percentage of black American respondents perceived most members of their group as well as themselves socially interacting with whites, at the same time black Africans seem to be blamed for their social interactions with whites. Why is this so? A possible answer is suggested in our next chapter, which deals with black male/female relationships.

7.
Nature and Extent of Respondents' Male and ———— Female Interactions

In this chapter we are going to examine a rather sensitive area of black American and African social relationships, those of males and females with each other and with whites.

First, let us try to identify who are the whites with whom the black groups claimed to interact socially. The respondents were asked, "Who are those whites you interact with socially?" (See Table 15.)

The data indicated that 54 and 50 percent of both groups of respondents interacted with their white "school/classmates." However, none of the black American respondents and 33 percent of African respondents indicated not only that the whites they socially interacted with were their school- and classmates but also that the relationships had gone beyond class and school. These had "girlfriends/boyfriends." Only 9 percent of the black Americans and 17 percent of the black African respondents indicated that some of the members of the white community with whom they interacted socially were "family friends." Fourteen percent of the black Americans and none of the black Africans indicated that some of the members of the white community with whom they interacted socially were their "teachers or bosses." Nine percent of black Americans did not respond to this question.

Again the data indicate that 50 percent of the black Africans do have white "girlfriends/boyfriends" and "family friends" as members of the white community with whom they interacted

TABLE 15

Whites with Whom Respondents Interact Socially

Responses	Black Americans		Black Africans	
	Number	Percentage	Number	Percentage
Inapplicable*	18		4	
School/classmates	12	54	18	50
Girl/boy friends	0	0	12	33
Family friend	2	9	6	17
Employer/teacher	3	14	0	0
Teammates	3	14	0	0
No response	2	9	0	0
Total	22	100	36	90

*The inapplicable data are not included in this table.
  Black Americans, N=22. Black Africans, N=36.

socially while none of the black American respondents indicated
this to be the case. Their social interaction relationships could
also imply more shallow, formal sorts of social relationships
than that of "family" or "boyfriend or girlfriend."

It is interesting to note that a considerable amount of discussion and criticism was hurled particularly at black American
males who were accused by black American females of dating
white girls at the expense of their black sisters. When this issue
was investigated further, it was pointed out and emphatically
stressed that such unions were considered offensive or even
harmful to the black community. These relationships were
considered detrimental to the whole concept of "black unity"
and solidarity, a "sell-out" of black identity. Most respondents
seemed to know of people they had labeled as "Uncle Toms"
who, as one respondent put it, "talk black but sleep white."

Let us examine next the circumstances under which they
interacted socially with whites identified as best friends. (See
Table 16.)

Those respondents who indicated that they did interact

TABLE 16

Circumstances under Which Respondents Interact Socially with Whites

Responses	Black Americans		Black Africans	
	Number	Percentage	Number	Percentage
Inapplicable*	18		4	
In school	17	77	1	2.8
On dates	0	0	5	13.9
At home	0	0	21	58.3
At work	3	14	9	25.0
During sports	2	9	0	
Total	22	100	36	100.0

*The inapplicable data are not included in this table.
  Black Americans, N=22. Black Africans, N=36.

socially with the members of the white community were asked
under what circumstances these social interactions occurred.
Among those who admitted social interactions with whites,
77 percent of the black Americans indicated that their social
interactions took place at "school," while only 2.8 percent of
the Africans indicated this to be the case.

None of the black Americans and 13.9 percent of the African
respondents indicated that their social interactions with whites
took place on "dates." None of the black American respondents
indicated that their social interactions with whites took place
at "home," while a relatively large number of the African
respondents, 58.3 percent, indicated this to have been true.
Fourteen percent of black American and 25 percent of African
respondents indicated that their social interactions with whites
took place at "work."

The data indicate that most black American respondents
who do socialize with whites tend to do so at "school," while
the Africans tend to do so under different social situations,
on "dates," at "home," and at "work." It is possible that some
black Americans who have lived in racially segregated social

conditions have never had the opportunity to meet and get to know their white counterparts who live in predominantly racially segregated residential suburban neighborhoods, where racial stereotypes abound. Most black Africans who come to these educational institutions tend to live and move around in academic social situations where racial attitudes might not be as negative as those often found when blacks attempt to move into exclusively white neighborhoods. American institutions of higher learning are often known and identified with more progressive racial attitudes than American society at large. Hence, the black African students on these campuses tend to hold closer social relationships with some members of the white academic community than their black American counterparts.

It should be pointed out, however, that during discussions it came to light that though most black African students said they did interact socially with whites, not all of them did so to the fullest extent. For example, nationality differences were noted. Among black African respondents, those who came from nations which were then still under colonial rule seemed to interact socially less with whites, for example, African students from South Africa, Namibia, Angola, and Mozambique.

African students from French-speaking countries tended to interact socially with whites more intimately than those African students from former British colonies. African females hardly ever socially interacted with non-Africans, white or otherwise. Their close friends were more often their American families, schoolmates, and/or roommates.

Several important undercurrents that seem to pervade black American and African social relationships need to be noted here.

First, the issue of relationships between black males and females was the only variable that divided the groups along sex lines rather than along nationality. From a distance, the relationships between black males and females appeared to be generally strained. For example, black females criticized black males for showing little or no interest in their own females. Black males' interest in females was perceived to be more often than not geared toward white females.

Black males, on the other hand, did not view themselves as interested exclusively in white or other nonblack females, but rather, they tended to describe themselves as men who have certain compelling male needs that needed to be met by females in general. They criticized black females for their unwillingness and/or inability to meet their masculine needs. Though most black males admitted to having white women as girlfriends, they did not concede this to be their fault, but rather placed the blame in black females' laps. Black females were viewed as the culprits who, in one way or another, drove black males to seek nonblack females.

Through long, often heated discussions, two social situations seemed critical in any discussions that had to do with the nature and extent of black male and female relationships that must be examined closely: dating and marriage situations.

It has already been pointed out that from a distance, black male and female social relationships seemed to be strained. The causes seemed to vary between sexes. In order to gain a better sense of black male and female relationships let us isolate and fine-tune them, examining them under dating and marriage conditions. When this was done, nationality differences emerged, again dictated by differences between two sets of cultural behaviors and expectations, one being generally described as African and the other as American and Western.

Before we examine the respondents' attitudes towards dating and marriage further, let us briefly examine the African traditional and the American Western family systems. By examining both of these family systems, it is hoped that it will give us a better insight and understanding about why the male and female relationships of these two groups of young blacks appeared frequently to be socially strained.

African Traditional and American Western Family Systems

An in-depth examination of both African and American family systems is beyond the scope of this book, but some distinctive features that generally characterize as well as distinguish both family systems shall be briefly highlighted here.

The American family system, which predominates in the Western world, is by nature and character a *nuclear family*. That is, the conjugal family unit generally consists of a husband, wife, and their dependent children.

The foundations of the African family system are deeply rooted within the African *extended family* system. That is, in Africa, unlike the Western system of kinship and marriage, the individual's rights and obligations are towards a larger community of kin than himself, his wife, and their dependent children. The extended family system extends the individual's rights, obligations, and responsibilities far beyond those characteristically assumed and expected under the American nuclear family system. The extended family may, and often does, engulf three or more generations of nuclear families of lineal descendants. In other words, it includes all the individual's relatives, both close and distant.

When the extended family is formally defined by sociologists and anthropologists, it refers to more than one nuclear family living together or very near each other under the headship of one person whose position of leadership is defined by rules of descent.[1]

A second feature that distinguishes African and American systems of kinship and marriage is *polygyny*. Polygyny is the marriage of one man to two or more wives at a time. This system of marriage has been practiced traditionally throughout the continent of Africa, and it is still practiced, with a few exceptions, especially among the few African elites, who by and large have been educated within the Western educational traditions and social milieu. They have assimilated some aspects of the Western life styles and have adopted a *monogamous* system of marriage practices.

Even though the modern African elites have adopted the Western monogamous system of marriage, there are strong indications that a man's choice to limit his marriage only to one wife does not diminish his larger rights, obligations, and responsibilities to his own extended family. Strong kinship ties to the larger extended family are still maintained.[2]

For example, a study conducted by this author indicated that among Nairobi's modern African elites, "going back home (in their rural homes of origins) on week-ends to visit their family and relatives" was named as their first choice of leisure activities. The same study indicated a higher propensity for many modern Kenyan nuclear family households to consist of more than one family in the urban areas. The African respondents, as opposed to Europeans, indicated a strong sense of obligation to "help" the many members of their extended family clan, both in rural and in urban areas. "Help" to kin ranged all the way from contributing goods and services to self-help schemes back home, to paying school fees for their relatives' children in urban areas, to providing room and board for relatives and friends temporarily seeking employment in Nairobi.[3]

Although from a distance most modern African urban elites' marital practices reflect a nuclear monogamous form of marriage, this feature can be deceiving at times. For most Africans, there is no guarantee that they will remain monogamously married throughout their entire lives. As they get older and become more economically secure, some, if not most, tend to marry other wives or keep mistresses. The fact that they appear to have one wife and their children under one roof does not dismiss the strong ties that exist between them and their kin both in town and in rural areas.

Though the American monogamous system of marriage implies marriage of one man to one woman at a time, and since this system is not conducive to multiple spouses at a time, individuals often resort to *serial marriage*, that is, divorce from one spouse in order to marry another.

A third distinction between the African and the Western marriage systems is the rule of residence.

In the United States, newly married couples are free to choose where they are going to live after marriage. They often can and do establish their own new residence separate and apart from both of their families of orientation. This freedom of choice to live apart from both of their families of birth is known as *neolocal*. The ability for the new couple to establish a new place of residence after marriage makes fewer demands on their economic and other obligations towards their kin at large. The young couple's living away from both their families of orientation affords them a certain degree of independence and privacy.

In African traditional systems of kinship and marriage, a *patrilocal* rule of residence is the most common feature. Here, characteristically, the bride moves from her own family of orientation and joins the groom and his family. The couple establishes residence with or near the groom's family.

There are other rules of residence in some parts of Africa such as *matrilocal*, where a male leaves his family of orientation to join his bride's family; the *bilocal*, where couples may live with either of their families; and the *avunculocal*, where the bride and groom live with or near a maternal uncle of the groom. Although these other forms of rules of residence exist in Africa, they are not dominant characteristics. We shall stress the patrilocal rule of residence because it is the most salient feature in most parts of Africa.

A fourth distinctive feature that generally sets the African extended family system off from the American nuclear family system is the rules of descent.

In the United States a *bilateral* rule of descent is a common feature. That is, children in a nuclear family can and may inherit and hold property from both sides of their families. Also, both sons and daughters may inherit and hold property in their own names as dictated by local customs that define the "closeness" or distance of relatives who may or may not qualify for family inheritance.

In Africa in general, as most societies tend to be patriarchal, a *partrilineal* rule of descent is pervasive. Here, family property is passed down from fathers to sons. Although children are by blood related to their own mother's family of orientation, they are often excluded from inheriting properties from their mother's side of the family.

Generally the African traditional system of kinship and marriage has a far stronger grip on the individual than the American one. By virtue of its far-reaching social extended family tentacles, it influences the individual's behavior and actions throughout life far more profoundly. On the other hand, although Americans are emotionally, by birth and marriage, tied to their kin, because of the basic right of individual independence they are not legally bound to their families. Although individuals may choose to listen to and obey their parents and other members of the family, through an occasional extension of a helping hand, this is nevertheless carried out more according to a person's willingness rather than as dictated by law.

The American system of marriage allows individuals the freedom to choose their own future mates. Typically, emphasis is placed upon "romantic love" as characterized and perpetuated by Hollywood. Mutual attraction carries a high social and emotional premium. Verbal demonstration of love and affection is expected. Physical demonstrations, too, in the form of hugging, holding hands, and kissing are part and parcel of being in love with someone. Although couples in love do inform their parents and relatives of their ultimate choice, if they are both of age the choice to marry or not to marry is legally left up to them to decide.

In most African traditional societies, marriage does not necessarily look to romantic love as its sole propelling force. Rather, it is often understood that love will grow as the young couple live together and get to know and understand one another more deeply. Verbal or public demonstration of love and affection is strongly discouraged. Marriage is considered to be such a serious undertaking as to warrant taking major marital decisions from the hands of the young and inexperienced. Therefore, it becomes a communal rather than an individual responsibility and concern.

Many societies throughout Africa allow the couple to live together before marriage. For instance, among the Kisii and Luos of Kenya, after a portion of a dowry has been given, the prospective bride is allowed to move in and live with her future husband and his family. This process is accomplished over several periods of time. This gives her a chance to examine and experience first-hand her relationship with her future family to see whether or not she will fit in with the rest of the family. After this trial period, both parties have a right to withdraw from the impending marriage if one or both believe that this marriage will not work out successfully. The portion of the dowry that had been given is returned without asking further questions. Africans do not marry individuals; rather, they marry from a family into another family. Therefore, an individual's character is weighed not only from the point of view of the two individuals' compatability but more importantly from whether or not a bride will be able to fit into an existing family structure. She is viewed from the larger community's perspective rather than from merely her own groom's view.

African families can and often do veto their sons' and daughters' mate choices. Not only do they have the right to do so, but they also have an obligation to state what they feel and think is going to be good for the community at large.

African families consult with their sons and daughters to make sure that prospective couples do like and consent to the marriage. This is paramount because family involvement does not start and end with the completion of the wedding ceremony but continues to be exercised to a certain degree throughout life. The family knows that if they force an unwilling individual into a marriage, when and if future marital problems develop, they would be held directly or indirectly responsible. It is in everyone's interest within the larger community to make sure that the marital match is the best one possible.

In many societies in Africa, the prospective groom's family offers the bride's family a dowry. It takes many forms, such as cows, goats, sheep, chickens, and the like. Currently, however, a few societies take equivalent monetary exchanges in lieu of the former tribal gifts.

The concept of "dowry" has often assumed, in most non-African people's minds, the appearance of a commercial transaction. To Africans, the gifts to a bride's family is not a commercial deal, nor is it a buying or selling of a bride. Rather, the gifts are intended to allow the future bride's brother to acquire a wife to take the place of his sister's departure to her family of procreation. As an American prospective groom's offer of a diamond ring to his future wife is not normally considered a "sale" or a "bribe," neither is the African dowry gift.

Having examined some salient features that distinguish the African traditional and the American Western family systems, we will now examine the male and female relationships between black Americans and Africans within this cultural context. We shall examine how they view their relationships in both dating and marriage situations.

The Dating Situation

BLACK AMERICAN FEMALE VIEWS ON DATING
BLACK AMERICAN MALES

First, let us start with how black American females view black males. Most black American females in this study preferred dating men of their own kind. Very few, if any, dated males from other racial groups. Overwhelmingly, black females said they preferred to date "brothers." Those who were not dating "brothers" even went without dating at all rather than date nonblacks.

Those who dated or had dated black males seemed somehow unsatisfied with their relationships. As one black American female explained, "they are cheap and often treat us like shit." Another sophisticated black American female respondent, who worked full-time but attended evening classes, said the following about black American males on dates:

> I am so tired of our men! They want to take you out but they do not want to spend any money on you. They ask you for a date, and guess where they will take you? To your own apartment. They will expect you to buy the food, cook it, serve them, and probably will drink your wine too, and then expect you to give them a good time. I am tired of giving men free rides and entertaining them. From now on, whenever one asks me for a date, it had better be a real one, or else I'll step on my gas pedal and take off in a cloud of smoke. Sometimes I don't understand if they really like and want me or is it my money, car, or apartment. I have decided to put an end to all this.

Another respondent quipped:

> The brothers will take us (black women) to a hamburger
> stand, while they save themselves and their money for
> their real date (white women) to take them to nice places.
> They only pay us lip service of all the black Sister shit and
> smile, while the real stuff is saved for his white girlfriend.

On the dating issue black American females were more critical
of their black American males. Black males were under vehement
attack for dating white females. Black females felt rather short-
changed by their males. At times, the discussion got rather
heated, where black males were accused of selling out the black
revolution. Black males were viewed, on one hand, as echoing
"black is beautiful" while, on the other, they were seen as being attracted by what black females called "ivory skins, blue
eyes, and blonde hair." Black males who dated white females
were characterized as "Uncle Toms" who "talk black but sleep
white."

If, indeed, the concept of black unity was ever going to become a reality, most black women felt that its roots lie deep
within the strengths of the black family. If black males are
deserting their own females for others, then there will be no
foundations on which a strong united black family will be
built and perpetuated.

Here, of course, in the middle of it all, the culprit perceived
to have come between black males and females is the white
female. Few black females express patience towards white
females who hunt for black males. Black females are certain to
express their feelings that parallel what Inez Reid's respondents
aptly expressed as follows:

> A black brother walking down the street arm in arm with
> a white woman—most of all a white hippie—can make a
> black woman ready to spit fire. The fire surfaces more
> rapidly when an accusatory glance in the direction of the
> brother brings no response other than a stone, expression-
> less face, or a slight smile which reads, "Yeah, I got her;

what you going to do about it?" The return glance, equally accusatory, reads: "I bet you rapped the loudest the other day about the honky, whitey, the white devil, and off the pig. Furthermore, she's ugly as sin."[4]

In the same passage, Reid gives us a psychological glimpse of the white girls who are caught in this dilemma on the psychological battleground of the Black sexes. To this a white girl remarked:

> The only bad thing I remember about being with him (a black male) was when we'd walk down the street and a black girl passed us. She'd look at me accusingly. At that moment I would gladly have traded my blonde hair and white skin for her dark looks. I felt ashamed and embarrassed.[5]

Reid poses a very puzzling question as to "why do black men, even in the day of black liberation still date, have affairs with, and even marry white women?" Some of the answers she gives range all the way from: black men seen as searching for "symbols of beauty" in white women, "yet time and time again Black men's 'symbol of beauty,' and will not rest until he has her safely entertwined in his arms, even if it's only for a night, a week, a month, or six months."[6]

Another reason advanced for the defense of the black male and white female intimate relationship is that "White women have positive effect in terms of making Black manhood a reality and easing the nervousness and anxiety of Black men.[7]

Here again, the white woman's image is larger than life. Some black females expressed their own feelings in the most articulate manner. Those black females who had things to say felt rather cheated by their black males. Black females felt that black males view them as cheap. The cheapness was not wholly measured in terms of economic standing, but rather in attitude. Black females felt somewhat cheated when black males did not date them while they dated white women. Those who ventured to date black females seemed to come out as cheap. The perceived tight-fistedness was translated to mean black males were somehow saving themselves and whatever resources they had for what was often described as a "real date"—white female dates. As one respondent put it:

> Brothers give us jive talks about the black revolution, black nationalism and black is beautiful jazz, until bedtime. They talk about all that but when it comes to bedtime, kiddo—they sleep white. Brothers don't seem to understand they need us as much as we need them. What we need to do is build a strong black family and, eventually, a black nation.

Though under dating situations there seem to be strains in the relationships, when it comes to marriage all the black American female respondents I talked to strongly felt and said they preferred to marry their own black males.

BLACK AMERICAN FEMALE VIEWS ON DATING AFRICAN MALES

Black American females' attitudes towards dating black African males, for those who dated across nationality lines, seemed to be relatively more favorable than towards black American males. To some black American females, in dating situations African males were viewed as "perfect gentlemen," and one respondent said, "They treat us like women." Then she added:

> The African guys are gentlemen. When they take you out, you know you will go out on a real date. They treat you like a woman should be treated. They take you to some of the nicest places in town and they are not afraid to spend their money in order to have a real good time.

Black African males were perceived to treat women with great care, love, respect, and dignity. Another respondent said,

"They've got class," and added, "The ones I know are real men in the truest sense of the word." Often black African males were characterized as less fussy in their social interaction patterns. They tended to try harder to make a woman happy, except for a few social and cultural fumblings that, in these cases, were often overlooked because "they were not used to our American dating game."

Black African males, unlike their American counterparts, were viewed as people who love to have a good time, and often the good times were demonstrated by taking black women out on "real dates." When further elaboration was sought as to what was meant by a "real good time" it seemed to comprise of special ingredients such as taking women to "nice places in or out of town to eat rather than out to hamburger stands and to new entertainment places where they could have a real good time." African males were viewed as not afraid to spend money in order to have a good time.

They were also described as being and acting more "mature" in general than non-African males of their age. Most of them were viewed as academically serious, almost bordering on intellectual fanaticism, and this intellectual seriousness was appreciated. At times, it did contribute to strains in relationships, when African males were viewed as too engrossed in their work as well as their passion for home and international political discussions at the expense of a good time.

Another flaw that seemed to emerge to mar the African male's otherwise "gentleman" image and was mentioned more often was that African males were generally "too fast." Specifically, black African male new arrivals were criticized for their inability to know when or when not to make a sexual move. Most of them were criticized for their inability to distinguish between "liking" and "loving" someone.

Here, too, there was a cultural difference of opinion between African attitudes towards love and marriage and those expected by American females. The Americans seem to distinguish differences between "liking" and "loving" someone, whereas the African views "liking" as a natural first step that, it is hoped, with time will grow and blossom into "love." On the whole,

Africans do not seem to give much social credence to instantaneous romantic love that, like a bolt of lightning, would strike an individual while leaving enough social and emotional momentum to sustain it through a married life that will last a lifetime.

Black American females stated that there was a vast difference between "liking" and "loving" someone, whereas black African males seemed to feel that the line between "liking" and "loving" someone was thin, if not indistinguishable. As one African respondent put it:

> There is no difference between liking and loving. It is a continuum. First you like someone, then when you get to know them better, you like them very much and then further down the line you eventually fall in love with them. It's a myth perpetuated by Hollywood. You might like someone the first time, still you must reserve your final sense of judgment for later, after you've known them a little bit better.

Black American females who had experienced going out on dates with Africans, particularly newly arrived Africans, seemed to feel a communication gap, albeit a cultural one. As one of the black American female respondents said:

> When I first went out on a date with X, he was so good and treated me like a queen, but later on he wanted me to spend the night with him. But, when I said no, he seemed shocked. He asked me why, I told him I liked him but I didn't love him, at least, not yet. Then he asked me point blank, if you didn't love me, why then did you agree to go out with me. I tried to explain it to him why but I don't think my explanations made any difference. He never asked me out after that though I think he liked or even loved me. And, on my part too, given time, I think I liked him a lot. I could see myself falling in love with him and even marrying him. But due to our cultural misunderstandings we've lost each other.

On the issue of cultural differences that seem to plague black American and African dating habits, one black American female who had lived and worked in Africa for several years had this to say:

> The first time I met and dated Africans, I had a lot of problems understanding their dating behaviors. It wasn't until I moved and lived in Africa for a while that I finally realized what was happening, and that there were very remarkable differences in terms of dating. For example, I had a hard time trying to reconcile what they and I expected after a date. But then when I was in Africa, I learned why. At first, when I got to Africa, African married men wanted to take me out on dates. When I reminded them that they were married, invariably they'd say, "What has being married got to do with us going on a date?" I just couldn't deal with it. Although somewhere in the back of my mind I knew that Africans practiced polygyny, the idea had really not sunk in.

The respondent related her own personal experience while in Africa, where she was faced with a married male who wanted to sleep with her in his own home with his own wife present. "The trouble was," she said, "they were my closest friends. Although I knew that married men everywhere try to sneak around behind their wives' backs, nothing had prepared me for what I would find in Africa. It was so open, so blatant and the males were so aggressive about it. I just couldn't deal with it."

Although black American females know that Africans can have more than one wife and that in many African societies a sexual double standard is often applied, black American females did not seem to understand this in light of their own cultural standards. The same respondent continued:

> My African family invited me to their home to spend a weekend with them. But when I got there, the husband started acting sort of strange. You know, showing me a lot of attention. I felt very uncomfortable. Then later, as

the evening progressed, he became even more agressive.
I rose to leave. They were both upset. His wife took me
in and assured me that it was o.k. for me to sleep with
her husband. This confused me even more. I nearly went
to pieces. By that time I was too upset to stay. So I left.

I was upset because the husband would even dare ask me
to sleep with him in his own home with his wife present.
I was even more upset that his own married wife would,
too, join in to encourage me to sleep with her own husband
right there in her presence. I felt very sorry for her. That
was only my first experience, mind you. Later, a lot more
followed just like that I have just related. After that I
concluded there was no reason for me to be constantly
upset. I realized their values and ours were very different
and if I was going to survive and come home sane, I decided
to accept them just the way they were. I realized that
there was nothing I was going to do to change them. You
either join them or you get out. So I decided to calm down
and let things just roll.

Another thing I learned that helped me was, if I knew I
did not want to go out or sleep with a man, I just didn't
accept any date from them, period. I had already learned
that to accept a date was also to accept the consequences
of a date afterwards, sex. It was just as simple as that. But
I had to learn it the hard way, by trial and error. It's
nothing that someone can tell you or teach you. It's something you must learn all by yourself. Now for me, it has
made things much easier and enjoyable to date African
males who are here. I understand them from home. Although most of them have also become westernized and
taken up some of our mores, still, I know and understand
them a little bit better than I did before going to Africa.

This particular young lady was planning to return to Africa to
get married and live there. After observing how polygynous
marriages work in Africa first-hand, she did not seem at all
worried should her future husband marry another wife. To this
she said:

Once they get into your blood, it's very hard to give them up and think of someone else. They are a beautiful people in every way. If I have to face a co-wife, it wouldn't faze me out one bit. When an African male marries another wife, it doesn't mean he does not love the first wife, on the contrary. So, now, I feel quite comfortable with them. I have accepted them and their culture completely. I know if I am going to marry and live with one, I'm emotionally prepared to accept his sleeping with other women and even marrying them.

This particular respondent's advice on how to deal with African males was sought by other black American females who dated and seemed to experience some difficulties with African males. To this she said,

Those sisters dating Africans need to have their heads screwed on straight. When they come to me for advice, I tell them they either will have to accept the Africans the way they are or leave them alone. Some of them are still very young. They get upset when Africans date them and then when they find the same men they think they love and who love them have other women on the side. I tell them, this practice is as old as history itself in Africa and that they should not try to change the African men, they should either change and accept them or leave them alone.

Here, the inherent problems for black American females dating African males seem to arise due to two different cultural modes of expectations and behaviors. African males felt that if a mature woman has accepted a date, then she should also be willing and able to accept what they thought were natural consequences of a date, sex. They seemed much more intolerant and impatient with the delicate dictates of what they called "the American dating game." To them, dating was merely a "game." Other males, on a lighter note, had coined a new term to refer to the "dating game"; they called it sexual "red tape." The "red tape" appeared to most of them to be a huge social master plan that dictated what should happen during the first, second, and nth date.

To most African males, the dating game was viewed as an intricate social machinery used by the system as a form of delay tactics. This system of sexual "red tape," they felt, had out-lived its usefulness and needed to be discarded under modern conditions. If two people loved and cared for each other, they didn't see why they had to follow some archaic system. All the relevant stages could and should be short-circuited. It should be noted that this was the only time when African males seemed to prefer modern emancipated women, because these women did not let their social lives be dictated by a long process of use-less steps that could eventually lead to what both parties, if they both mutually liked and cared for each other, expected to finally reach, sex. They rather preferred things to take their own natural course and happen spontaneously, because, they felt, spontaneity was a mirror of life.

American females who dated African males also indicated that they experienced difficulties in dating African males. The African males seemed evasive sometimes. The women did not seem to know whether they were loved ones or whether they were just mere females who also happened to be very good friends. They found African males difficult to pin down with regard to their short-term or long-term relationship plans, whether they were in love with or just liked them.

What, to most black American females, seemed to be the evasiveness and inability of African males to express what they emotionally felt towards black females, some of it if not most, can be explained through cultural differences, as has been indi-cated. Often Africans' decision to marry is not a unilateral decision taken independently, but rather, a family affair. Often, most African males hold the request and commitment for marriage abroad until they have tested the family waters back home.

Most African young men and women abroad are under strict family orders not to marry anyone from abroad. This includes even other Africans from different nations, tribes, or clans that are not within an individual's direct line of marriage. It is true

that some Africans have married abroad. Most of them, however, married mates of their choice, despite immense social
pressures from home. When they choose to marry anyone
without the blessings of the extended family back home, they
do so at the risk of future social strains with their extended
family and even of social ostracism, by virtue of breaking their
social rules of *endogamy*, or marriage within the group that an
individual is supposed to marry from or into.

Another aspect that may contribute to an American female's
lack of knowledge of whether or not she was "loved" or just
"liked" is the Africans' traditional culture's discouragement of
public demonstration and expression of love and affection. For
example, an African and a black American female had a wonder-
ful time together and the man acted truly fond of her. When
they met each other, he acted as if she were only a casual
schoolmate, or worse still, as if she did not exist at all. Such
experiences more than baffled non-Africans, or those who did
not know or understand Africans well. A free-wheeling demonstration of love and affection in public can, and does, embarrass
most, if not all Africans.

When a non-African female was as demonstrative as she was
accustomed to being, she was, with few exceptions, likely to
get socially rebuffed. She was likely to be outraged and conclude that he did not care for her as much as she thought he did.
In reality, the private story in his heart was often different.
He could, in his heart, love and care for her deeply. Love and
affection of one human being for another is not a public show.
Physical or verbal public demonstrations of love and affection
more often than not are viewed by the African as definite
signs of either immaturity or insecurity, and often both.

BLACK AMERICAN MALES' VIEWS ON DATING
BLACK AMERICAN FEMALES

Black American males expressed resentment at black American females under dating situations. Black American males felt
that a black woman would be one of the worst possible females

a man could possibly want to take out on a date. Black females
were generally characterized as "difficult to date." On this
issue one black American male had this to say about black
women in general:

> Black women are shit, man. You have to go through so
> much shit and crap, man, in order to date a sister [black
> woman]. Why in the hell should I go through all that crap
> when I don't have to? Tell me, Why? sisters are shit!
> Sisters better get themselves together and come to their
> senses or else! They will have to go to bed with a hot water
> bottle or a pillow to cuddle for the rest of their damn
> lives! You ask me why? The simple reason I date white
> chicks [white girls] is plain and simple: they make and
> treat you like a man. And, I will tell you again, sisters are
> shit, man!

Although some black American males dated white females,
most black American males dated black American females.

As in the situation where black Africans were blamed for
associating with whites to a higher degree, black American
males, more often than not, were blamed for dating non-black
American females. Rarely, if ever, did black American females
come under the same attack for dating white males.

Since most black American males dated and eventually
married black American females, many males had many good
things to say about black women. As one black American male
respondent indicated:

> We owe them our full respect, lives and sanity. They are
> the ones who have kept our black family and helped us to
> survive over these years. Whether we like it or not, they
> are ours and we are theirs. What we see now is, growing
> up pains. Most of us will eventually get over it. If we
> followed our African traditional lifestyles and shake off
> the whiteman's ways, we should get along with one an-
> other just fine. And getting along we must. If nothing else
> but for the sake of our own black revolution and eventual
> survival of the black people on this world.

Despite what appeared to be strained relationships between black American males and females, most black males respected their females. It appeared that most of the existing social strains had something to do with the problems of the American "dating game." As one black American male respondent added:

No matter what brothers say, sisters don't like being hustled. They don't like being used either. They like honesty and sincerity. Sisters are not fools, they're way ahead of us brothers. They want respect from brothers. Is that too much to ask from one human being to another? I don't think so. Personally, I think we brothers have alot of learning to do from our sisters. They seem to have got it together much better than we have. If we stopped and listened to them for a while, at least, I think it can help us all get our heads together. Personally, I love sisters. I can't claim to speak for every brother but I'll stick to my own kind. It makes a lot of sense. Sisters are the best thing that ever happened to us black brothers.

Most black American males indicated that they had never dated an African female. Some of them said even the thought of dating an African female had never really even crossed their minds, let alone considering them as possible future mates. It should be stressed here again that there were very few black African females on these campuses. It was noted, however, that black American males were close friends with African women. When these men were asked whether or not they dated African females, they all without exception indicated that they had never considered asking their African female friends out on a date. When asked why, the responses were uniform. "The thought of it had just never crossed my mind. I never stopped to think about it," one black male said.

It appeared that the relationships between black American males and African females were friendly and warm. It lacked social strains that seemed to pervade in other relationships. It is believed that this was due to black American males' failure to consider African females as possible dates or marriage partners and to the African females' nonparticipation in American dating practices.

Black American males seemed to air the same difficulties experienced by the Africans in dating black American females. They, too, like black African males, seemed anxious and impatient concerning the general American dating habits and customs, although they had not coined an elaborate term to describe the dating process. Nevertheless, there were many instances where they felt or expressed a strong sense of frustration at the social machinery of the "dating game."

Particularly incensed were black American males who had a strong Afrocentric view. To these, the Americans' general "dating game" was only one characteristic of the dominant white society's social and cultural imperialism used to control individual and group free expression of emotions. According to their male counterparts, black American females seemed to suffer from these general symptoms of social and cultural "up-tightness" that needed to be discarded in preference for the African traditional extended family forms.

Black American females are viewed as culprits who drive their male counterparts into laps of nonblack American females and should have no reason to complain when their males go elsewhere for female companionship and love. Black American females were generally characterized as slow to respond and at times seemingly uninterested; they were said to demand too much and expected too much.

When black American females were asked to comment on this issue, most of them indicated that they wanted to be treated with love, respect, and dignity.

BLACK AFRICAN MALE VIEWS ON DATING
BLACK AMERICAN FEMALES

First of all, most African males seemed to enjoy the "American dating game." Those who seemed to have little difficulty in dating seemed to have a good time. Here they were, very few of them, and on most American campuses, often the ratio between men and women is unbalanced in favor of males. Second, African males, despite racial attitudes, seemed to hold an advantage, as do other foreign males, over American males. They were often viewed, rightly or wrongly, as exotic. Third, evident also, history seemed to be on their side; the sweet taste of former African sons of chiefs, who in the olden days were the only ones who could afford to educate their sons abroad, seemed to linger on. Some African males took advantage of this. Fourth, in relation to their numbers, African males seemed to enjoy a relatively higher economic as well as social status than their counterparts, perhaps because some held generous government scholarships from their home countries, while others had attained advanced degrees which afforded them a higher occupational status than other students. Because of these conditions, perhaps coupled with others, they seemed to be better off than their black American male counterparts.

Black African males overwhelmingly preferred dating white females to any others. Before we go any further with this discussion, let us look at what they say about black American women in dating situations.

African males shared some negative feelings towards dating black American females with their American counterparts. As one respondent aptly put it:

> Black women are so proud, and conceited they think they are the God's own given blessing to man. They don't understand us men and the problems we have as men. They have to play their usual games (hard to get) and once you have managed to date her, the Black woman (specifically) wants a real date. A real date to them means precisely, picking her up at her place if you have a car, if you don't own one, then you'd better rent one or take a taxi. They want you to drop them at the door of the most expensive cocktail lounge in town. Here, pre-dinner cocktails should be served, then, if the cocktail lounge does not have a classy restaurant, then call another taxi to take them to one. Here she will have her classy meal in the real sense of the word. Some of them, more often than not, do not

even know what they are ordering. They just look at the
most expensive items on the menu and hope it is to their
liking. They start at the top of the menu and eat their
way down, while washing the dinner down with the most
expensive, imported wine. If it's local, it isn't as good.
Then she will have dessert, coffee, and liquor. After all
this, her evening has just started. She will suggest the most
expensive night spot in town for dancing with a floor
show; and to be sure of this, she makes sure the place has
a cover charge. While inside, of course, you will have more
drinks. And after all this, she might even decide she is not
in the mood for dancing! When she is through, she might
even suggest another expensive place for a snack, and
after this, another cab to her doorstep. Then when she is
through the door safely, only then does she shout back a
good-night, without even looking back, and, mind you,
she might even forget it altogether! And even before you
know it, you are cleaned out of your little cash you have
been saving to buy books or for rent. Also, mind you,
she still expects you to continue doing this indefinitely
before you even get your money's worth back [sexual
favors].

Black African males seem to resent the fact that the old
myths about all Africans coming from royal families are still
very strongly held or suspected by black American females.
They want to associate them with the black African like
"Black Cinderellas" in hope some day an African Prince will
come along to sweep them off their feet. The black African
males said that they had tried to dispel African royalty myths,
but said they were not given a chance to do so. However, some
of the black African males said they did take advantage of
royalty myths while they were here and while the myths lasted.
One of the respondents said:

American women seemed to be attracted by royal splen-
dor rather than personality magnetism, material gain rather
than individual worth. I have tried to tell them that I am in
no way a royal prince, that I am a son of an ordinary

African traditional family, a poor farmer's son, but they have refused to accept me the way I really am. So, I am going to play the game as long as it lasts. But, when the time comes for marriage, I'll go back to my own village and marry a real woman (one who respects her husband and one who does not dominate in the real African sense). How can I take one of these women (black American females) home to my mother? They don't have any respect for their parents, let alone their elders! If I took one of these home, I already know what the end results will be. She is bound to open her big mouth and tell my mother off, and act jealous and possessive of me and the children and the next thing I know is that I might end up in jail, a mental institution, or something similar. She will take the next plane out of the country as so many of them have done previously. They might be good for keeping me company while I'm here, but not to have them for keeps and to take home to Africa.

Obviously, this is a somewhat extreme case. However, it is also relatively true that in general, though the black African males seem to like liberated women, they do not appreciate their sense of independence and assertiveness. The black American women too, find it difficult when their African males cannot swear off polygyny. It creates in them a sense of insecurity that maybe these men will marry them and take them to Africa only to marry additional wives. They do not know where they would stand if this were to happen to them. Possessiveness and jealousy on the part of American women frighten African males. Demands by American women for goods and services and the belief that they ought to come before everyone else in the lives of their African males seem to cause male and female social strains.

BLACK AFRICAN MALE VIEWS ON DATING
WHITE FEMALES

A relatively larger number of African males dated white women, especially during the early 1960s. However, during the

time this study was being conducted, it was noted that black
African males were dating, and often married, black American
females.

However, during the time this study was being conducted,
there were several black African males married to white women.
Most of them were Europeans. Relatively few African males
dated white women exclusively. Others, however, dated women
of all races, deliberately refusing to acknowledge racial or nationality restraints.

Those black African males who dated white females were
asked why, and most of them said the following:

> The white girls may be white on the outside but they are
> human beings inside, and that's all I care about. They do
> understand us men; people like myself. They are honest,
> straightforward, and to the point. Once they have liked
> you, you know they have. With white girls we can both
> have a hamburger, french fries, and a coke, all for less than
> a dollar for both of us. If I ran short of cash, and she has
> some, she does not hesitate to spend it on both of us.
> While the black woman's friendship ends where your cash
> ends, white girls can do things for and with me. If a white
> girl likes me that I know, I am sure it is because of me,
> and it is real. I am sure she would not like me for my
> money because I do not have that much. Maybe for my
> looks, but again, this is for her to decide. As a matter of
> fact, white women have so much at stake for them to
> lose by being associated with me as a black man, but still
> I have nothing but real and genuine praise for the white
> girls. Most of them for being considered "piggy banks"
> (financial economic source) or "pleasure units" (sex as
> seen on an exploitive basis) are also tremendous pleasure
> to be with as companions. They are intellectual, besides
> the pleasure of having her, you can also enjoy the pleasure
> of her mind. I do not care what you think, feel or say
> right now, I am all for white girls until and unless a black
> woman of the same calibre comes along, I will do what
> they call "talking black, and sleeping white."

In general, white females were viewed as "understanding" of males' problems. They were viewed as generous and considerate. Besides expected feminine attributes that females bring into a relationship, white females were exceptionally viewed for their intellect, the ability to discuss their own ideas and feelings calmly. Also, there seemed to be a type of honesty and sincerity attributed to white women rather than to their black American counterparts. This, it seemed, was arrived at because, given the racial situation in America, no white woman, unless she was genuine, would want to mar her own reputation by associating with black males unless she seriously meant it. Some African males who dated white females even went as far as counting black/white marital unions that had succeeded and flourished back home and those with black American females that had failed. The same respondent added:

> I do not understand why the intermarriage among the African males and American white females seems to work out as opposed to the ones that involve black American females and African males. One would think it should be the other way around, but in practice, it is not.

BLACK AFRICAN MALE VIEWS ON DATING AFRICAN FEMALES

Black African males said that African women were the worst possible dates a male could wish to have. First, most African females did not go out on dates in the American sense of the word. The black African female was seen as being "primitive." Here, primitive was equated with the adherence to African traditions, customs, and practices. Some of them had never even conceived of ever going out on a date, let alone to go out with a male all evening, alone! Even when they learned to like a male, they preferred to have the relationship stop at its platonic stage. Most of them did not allow holding hands, putting arms around each other, kissing, light or heavy petting, not to speak of sexual relations. In general, they were said to be quite reserved and generally emotionally cold. This type of woman, males felt, was bound to sink all the financial and emotional resources a man could offer, with no results in sight.

One of the major problems that caused strains between African males and females was the fact that African males out-numbered African females by far. Because African females did not date much, coupled with keen competition for the few females who were around, African males found it necessary to turn elsewhere for dates.

Those African females who ventured out on dates still pre-ferred to be in the company of African males, but with one catch—often in groups, rather than alone. Those African women who went out on dates alone were engaged to be married to the man they were dating.

For dates, African males seemed to have written off their own African females. African females were viewed as a good source for unneeded headaches. Though African males had written off African females as potential dates, they nevertheless felt affectionately close to and protective of them.

THE AFRICAN FEMALE DATING SITUATION

It has already been noted that there were very few African females and that those few rarely dated. To non-Africans, the African females appeared to be a mysterious entity. They felt free to talk about their observations of both dating and marriage.

First of all, African females viewed the American dating game as a socially legitimatized process for easy sexual access for the unmarried. When asked how they had managed to survive with-out dating in a social climate where dating was an accepted pastime, and how did they respond to those males who asked them out for dates, one African female had this to say about how she dealt with non-African men:

> With non-African men it is easier to deal with them when they ask me out on a date. I go out with them. But when they start getting ideas, I establish my position right from

the very start. I tell them all my African taboos and sometimes, I even lie, you know! They do not know the difference. After all, what do they know about Africa? By the
time he has listened to all the do's and don'ts of African
traditions and customs, if he was solely after me for what
he could get from me usually by the end of the evening
and by the time I shake his hand at the door to say good-
night, I figure he has got the message. He will never come
back for more lectures on African customs and traditions.
And you know, most of them do not return after that
very simple test I use. The ones who are really interested
in me for myself will usually come back for more. The
American men are rather nice about this, they do not
argue with me; for, what is there to argue about? If they
do, I simply tell them it is against my African customs to
do this and that and I'm not ready or willing to break my
customs and traditions for them or anyone else. This
seems to put a certain form of finality to the whole thing
in this nature. I do not want to encourage them to do
something I'm not ready to do. I do not play games,
either. I mean what I say and I am very serious about it.

When the same respondent was asked her opinion of the black
African males, she had this to say:

African men are strange. They are among the most difficult
lot to deal with, and it is rather hard for me to understand
them. Here I am thinking that since they are from home,
they will be able to understand me better, but somehow,
they don't. I think something happens to the African
men as soon as they get off that plane from home. They
want to see me and treat me as they treat other women.
They know I am not an American woman. They tell me
I should act "civilized" (morally liberated). They seem
to equate "civilization" and "education" with immorality. As a matter of fact, African men are like chameleons.
They change their actions to suit their own liking and
convenience. For instance, when it comes to certain issues

which might undermine their status as males, they adhere
to and defend it with all the African traditions available
to them. On other situations they are so "civilized" and
so "Westernized" more so than Western man, himself.
There are so many African men here, and we are so few
African females that it would be unfair to date just one
of them. They are all very nice and I like all of them
equally. They treat me like a sister and they are all my
brothers.

Although African females do not date in general, there are
indications to show that the longer they remain in the United
States, the more likely they are to date American style. Young-
er females from African urban areas who have been exposed to
the Western way of life also tend to date.

As the African continent contains predominantly patriarchal
societies, female social and moral standards are watched more
closely and reinforced more forcefully than those that pertain
to males. African families keep a tight reign on their daughters
abroad through correspondence and through relatives and
friends who visit abroad. Friends travelling abroad are often
asked to check on how daughters are doing. It is not unusual
for African parents to try to recall their daughters home if they
hear she is getting romantically involved with someone abroad.

Marriage Situations

BLACK AMERICAN FEMALE VIEWS ON MARRIAGE

Almost all black American females unequivocally stated that
they preferred marrying a man of their race. The only problem
that seemed to pervade among them was the fact that some
doubted whether they would manage to find a black man of
their choice. Most of them seemed to feel that most attractive
black males were either already married or engaged or dating
nonblack women. They often viewed as "lost causes" the

formation of foundations for a strong black family that most of these respondents aspired to.

They also expressed great disappointments with black African males. African males were, more often than not, viewed as "less serious" when it came to marriage. As one female put it:

African males like to have us [black American females] for a good time. But when the chips are really down, Africans split fast to marry their own African females or white girls. They really don't want to bother with us as future mates.

Though the relationships between black males and females sound negative, when most blacks married they overwhelmingly tended to marry other blacks. It was true that several black males, both African and black American, were married to or planned to marry white women, but they were very few indeed.

These black American females who socially interacted with and dated black African males did not mind marrying Africans. As a matter of fact, despite the social strains perceived between these groups, it was noted that among the total African married males the majority were married to black American females. Their marriages seemed to be as happy as any other.

Also, there were several black American females who were in love with and intended to marry Africans. Most looked forward to eventually becoming a part of their African heritage where, they felt, they rightly belonged.

The only thing that seemed to cause some apprehension was the thought that perhaps in the future, their husbands might want to marry another wife. Though black American females had learned about the African polygynous system of marriage generally accepted and practiced in most African societies, few could persuade themselves to accept the practice for themselves. They viewed it more or less as an abstraction that would have nothing to do with them. To protect themselves, some had even gone as far as extracting a promise from their prospective husbands to swear off the African practice of polygyny.

BLACK AMERICAN MALE VIEWS ON MARRIAGE

When it came to marriage, black American males seemed to have little difficulty in choosing a mate. Their problem, unlike those experienced by their female counterparts, were not so much a lack of a suitable pool of eligible women to choose from, but rather, of having to choose only one from among many.

Despite social strains that seemed to plague both groups in dating situations, when it came to choosing a mate, black American males had a wide range of selection. For example, college and university educated black males often found themselves at the center of fierce competition from black females. The fact that black males knew that they were keenly sought after by females both on dates and as future mates contributed a large share of strain to dating situations. Their general attitude appeared to be nonchalant. They knew they could name their price.

Some of them, especially those who were good-looking and bright and came from good, well-established families, could afford to sit back and watch females, both black and white, compete for their love and affection.

Black American males preferred to marry their own black American females. They liked and admired black American females as future wives because, they said, "They are strong and capable of holding the family together."

Though some black American males dated white females, they viewed this merely as a stage of growing up in their own lives. When it came to marriage, however, they all preferred and intended to marry black women. None of the black American male respondents said they hoped or planned to marry white females.

BLACK AFRICAN MALE VIEWS ON MARRIAGE

Although African males seemed to have written off African females as dates, when it came to marriage they all named African females as their first choice as marriage partners. African males felt strongly that although African females made lousy dates, they made ideal wives. Although they were viewed as less understanding of male problems on dates, when it came to marriage, they stood at the top of the list for their deep understanding of their males. Also, African females were viewed as "feminine" women who knew and understood their feminine role in the home and society at large.

A double standard seems to pervade both African males and females. African males felt rather safe to reserve their African females for marriage because they knew that when it came to marriage, African females would be there, intact. As much as there seemed to be social strains and experiences among them during dating situations, they still had a very closeknit brotherly and sisterly love and affection. Both groups were overly protective of one another. Africans will look out for each other's welfare and interests despite social strains. It is, in a sense, the traditional African extended family obligation that both groups of Africans knew so well. It was something similiar to sibling rivalry, where one does not have to like or love brothers or sisters in order to help them, as one has a strong sense of family obligation towards them.

African males' second choice for a marriage partner went to any non-African female who possessed African women's qualities. When they were asked to enumerate the African women's fine qualities they liked, it proved rather difficult to list them. Although it was difficult to enumerate good African women's qualities, nonetheless, we can perhaps gain some insight into those general women's qualities African males alluded to that they did not like. For instance, African males did not like "loud, pushy" women (assertive), particularly those who disagreed with or contradicted their men in public. Though they enjoyed dating, women who dated many and different men were viewed as good for fun but never to be considered as potential future mates. Rather, they were clearly viewed as "bad" women. On the other hand, African females, who were viewed as the worst dates, were now on a premium list exclusively reserved for marriage as wives and as mothers of their children. Here, too, was any non-African woman who displayed qualities considered to be close to the African woman's qualities. When Africans, both male and female, approved any outside union, the individual concerned was said to be "so nice, she is just like an African."

Also, it was not unusual that most African males did not seem to like any of their African women who were said or who they felt to be "Americanized" or "Westernized" in a moralistic sense. Any who displayed such social traits or were "morally loose" in their dating habits were quickly removed from that special category of "good" African women in the pool of possible marriage partners and placed into the larger pool of those women whom African men could date but not marry. Thus, African women should be well-educated and probably embrace some qualitatively selected desirable "Western" social traits. But somehow, deep inside, she must also be, or at least reflect, some of those African qualities that are communally admired. Otherwise, she was no better than her Western, black or white, female counterparts who were considered to be "bad" girls.

Black African males also disliked in black American females their preoccupation with racial matters. As one respondent said, "They (black women) seem to have little that tickles the mind except talk about race, race, race. . . . There are more problems in the world besides racial ones, you know."

And yet, race, ancestry, and color are bonds that unite the two groups. Most American women were committed to social issues, especially those that affect blacks in America in particular and other blacks around the world in general, whereas most Africans reserve their energies for studies and expounding international politics. That was where, it seemed, American white females surpassed black American females, in their ability to be more than just sexual partners. They were able to discuss matters of general interest besides and beyond racial issues.

BLACK AFRICAN FEMALE VIEWS ON MARRIAGE

Black African females, like their male counterparts, had no question in their own minds whom they would like to marry—African males. Unlike the African men, they did not seem to have a second-best choice.

One of the reasons they gave, besides shared culture and traditions, was that they eventually wanted to return to Africa. To them, marrying anyone not African would mean living somewhere else other than Africa. When the question was raised of non-African males who might be willing to marry and move back to Africa, they seemed to feel that it might be hard for a non-African to adjust easily to the African way of life.

Here, too, was a strong indication that African females adhered to patriarchal and patrilocal family rules of descent and residence. They indicated that it would be difficult, if not socially awkward, to marry and take a non-African husband home to live, rather than the other way around.

Did African females resent African males' American dating habits? African females said they did not mind their males dating women, white or black. Somehow, they too tended to see this as a male's necessary and natural need. It was good and healthy for them, as long as their men did not expect them to do the same. It might be added here that African females as well as African males seemed to reflect and accept a certain "double standard." It was all right for their males to date in order to meet their masculine needs. They did not, however, insist that they were entitled to the same privileges.

This fact can be attributed to their own African cultural upbringing that allows males a sociocultural license to marry as many wives as he wishes, whereas the females are not allowed the same privilege. Although these African women had lived and studied in the United States over a long period of time and had been exposed to feminism, their overall attitudes towards sex, marriage, and women's roles in society were still characteristically traditional and African.

African males' attitudes towards sex, marriage, and male roles, too, tended to reflect strongly those derived from traditional African family systems, where males are likely to make the major decisions affecting their own families. The concept of feminism seemed to have touched them tangentially, and even the slight touch was still largely theoretical rather than in practice. When it came to practice, more often than not, they tended to be staunchly African in outlook.

It might be noted here, too, that the strong sense of freedom African women seem to allow their male counterparts, to date and even marry non-African women, could be explained as follows: In Africa in general, very well educated single African women are few and highly sought after as prospective wives. The competition to marry is very keen, and these women know it. Educated African males with a string of high degrees from the leading educational institutions around the world are fairly common. Single African women being educated abroad know that they do not have to concern themselves with searching for eligible African males here. When they go back home to Africa, they will have a wide choice of eligible African males to choose from. When they seem somewhat nonchalant about their males, it is believed that it is not a result of liberal thinking, but rather comes because they know they have that wide choice of premium African males waiting for them back home. Black American females seem to express that eligible black male bachelors of high caliber that would attract these well-educated, highly sophisticated black females are few. Those few seem to date white females at the expense of their black females.

Also, African females did not seem to mind which race their males dated. They seemed to view all American females as "American women," since both participated and followed the "American dating game." However, African males could date any female they wished, so long as they were considered "good" women. African females seemed to care and worry over the possibility of African males socially being corrupted by American "bad" women, and possibly being physically hurt in romantic triangles, such as being shot at by jealous lovers or their lovers' admirers. It should be noted that, during this time, the African community was feeling rather sensitive because of reports that had travelled across the nation of African males shot and killed over romantic affairs. As one African female recalled, "These American women can shoot a man without even blinking an eye. I do not believe an African woman would shoot a man. At least, I never heard any ever doing so for such a silly and stupid little thing like love." Though African females did not mind African males dating women American style, as long as those women they dated were perceived to be "good women," when it came to marriage, African females felt that their males should marry their own. It was better and easier for cultural reasons, above all else.

While African females seemed to give their males a free dating license, since dating was viewed as a temporary solution to male sexual needs, they frowned on those who married non-Africans. There were occasions, however, when those who did marry non-Africans were forgiven, if that person was somehow "worth" crossing racial or nationality barriers. In an attempt to determine what were the basic ingredients that made a person worth crossing the lines for, it was discovered that there were no particular ground rules to be followed in recruitment of future mates. Some factors can be roughly summarized, but even these are not rigidly followed. They consist of some of the following aspects: (1) worth in functional substance, for example, a woman who is extremely well educated or well talented in some aspects of her life that could contribute to some aspect of her husband's life and that of their future community; (2) she should be someone who is considered "good" in her moral character, particularly a woman who likes people and is very considerate of her husband, his friends, and other people in general; and, (3) probably be also fairly good looking, but looks alone are not considered to be a paramount ingredient.

The Africans, both male and female, seemed to disapprove of any African male or female who marries a "societal reject." Their philosophy seemed to be that, if one crosses lines for a bride, then she should be "the best." They did not seem to like the idea of, for instance, some white girls who have been socially rejected by their white males for one reason or other coming to the Africans in search of husbands. This prompted a Swahili-speaking male respondent to quote a Swahili proverb: "*Ukimla nguruwe, ni heri umchaguwe aliye mnono.*" ("If you eat a pig, you may as well choose the fattest." [since Moslems prohibit the eating of pork.]) As long as the chosen ones were the best possible recruits, it did not seem to matter much whether they were black American, white American, European,

Asian, Latin, or any other. What goes on when the brides are taken home is another matter, to be considered elsewhere.

Conclusions

First, we have a rift between black African males and females when caught up in the strange, but tantalizing, "American dating game," for which elaborate social norms and behaviors exist. Adjustment to the "dating game" proved especially difficult for African females. African males adjusted more readily or were at least able to fumble along, causing problems in ways in which each group viewed the other either as seeming to fit or not.

Second, the rift between black American males and females was stated in clear terms. The white female is viewed as having come between black American males and females.

If black American and African personal lives are as strained as they sound, should we then conclude that they are beyond repair? I think not. First, it should be noted, most of these young people are still quite young. In other young people of their age, are male/female relationships free of strain? Hardly. Therefore, this can be viewed as a phase which most young people go through that these respondents were going through. Despite what the respondents said about one another, in the end most of them dated and eventually married one another. Hence, their routine growing pains should not be misconstrued in any way as a permanent situation. It is not. For, when it comes down to chosing a mate to spend the rest of their lives with, all respondents from both groups chose to marry their own kind, to be the father or mother of their children. Most young people lead different lives while dating from those that they want and expect from marriage. Marriage means a choice of one individual among many with whom one chooses to spend the rest of his or her life. All these respondents, whomever they dated, still wanted to fall in love and eventually marry one of their own. This, in its own right, is a positive sign for all black young men and women.

Notes

1. Communications Research Machines, Inc., *Society Today*, 2nd. edition (Del Mar, California: Communication Research Machines, 1973), p. 294.

2. Kenneth Little, *West African Urbanization: A Study of Voluntary Associations in Social Change* (Cambridge: Cambridge University Press, 1966). Also, Josephine M. Moikobu, "Voluntary Associations and Leisure Activities in Nairobi," Nairobi, Kenya: Institute for Development Studies Sessional Paper No. 85, 1970.

3. Josephine M. Moikobu, "What Makes the Urban African Elites Run?: A Sociological Exploratory Study from Kenya". A paper presented to the Fall Regional Social Science Research Council, Graduate School and University Center, New York University, December 13, 1975. p. 11.

4. Inez Reid, *"Together" Black Women* (New York: Emerson Hall Publishers, Inc., 1972), p. 79.

5. Rosemary Santini, "Black Man: . . . as Seen Through White Eyes," *Essence*, July 1970, p. 12.

6. Reid, *"Together" Black Women*, pp. 79-80.

7. Ibid., p. 80.

Conclusion

The Study's Findings

The purpose of this study was to investigate whether or not
black Americans and Africans socially interact with one another.
Specifically, the study attempted to discover the basis, nature,
and extent of interaction between black Americans and Africans
by examining two major premises: the Eurocentric view and
the Afrocentric perspective.

Specifically, Chapter 1 dealt with the Eurocentric view of
black American and African identity and relations. Proponents
of the Eurocentric view maintained first that black Americans
have no distinctive cultural creations of their own;[1] whatever
sociocultural patterns black Americans reflect have come from
their larger American society, predominantly white and Western; and any sociocultural patterns that do not seem to fit
comfortably within the larger framework of Western civilization are deviant and are considered part of the black American
slave experience in the South or the urban ghetto experience
in the North.[2]

Second, the Eurocentric view maintained that, in general,
black Americans and Africans do not interact socially with one
another. Any social interactions between black Americans and
Africans are characterized as usually "strained."[3]

The Afrocentric perspective in Chapter 2, contrary to the
Eurocentric view, indicates that distinctive black American

sociocultural creations do exist; the distinctive black American sociocultural patterns that exist within certain segments of the black community are not necessarily "pathological" or "deviant"; the distinctive sociocultural creations did not come only as a result of blacks' existence in northern urban ghettoes or the slave plantations in the South; the distinctive black American sociocultural patterns are both viable and healthy; and they are not characteristics of a sick culture but rather have distinctive origins within the African continent.[4]

The Afrocentric perspective maintains that social interactions between Africans and black Americans do exist and are not "strained" because of problems between the two black groups but rather as a result of interactions with whites.[5]

Chapter 3 examined literary works that illustrate the emotions, feelings, tone, and various definitions both by black Americans and Africans of themselves, their world, and others. The mood and tone of people writing from different continents clearly indicated a longing for their cultural past roots.

The results from the study of 80 black American and African students in Chapter 4 indicated their complex identifications with one another. The findings of what the respondents felt they had in common with each another indicated that they shared common identities based either upon external (political, social, and economic) or internal (color/ancestry) dimensions. More Africans felt that they had internal dimensions of identity with their brothers and sisters in America, whereas more black Americans felt they had external dimensions of identity in common with Africans. They all did agree that, in one way or another, they are definitely one people.

The results from data concerning the national dimension of identity also revealed that the majority of the respondents from both groups felt that black Americans should be identified with Africa. Black Americans expressed their strong desires to immigrate someday to Africa to live should they have an opportunity to do so. They were emphatic in choosing to study in a university in Africa rather than in other universities from a list of five different continents given them.

Concerning the most salient characteristics liked and admired about one another, the respondents indicated overwhelmingly positive responses. Black Africans liked and admired their black American brothers' and sisters' sense of "black pride," their superior athletic, musical, and rhythmic endowments, their sense and will that had enabled them to survive this long and this far, their open-mindedness and outspokenness, their ease of communication, and their generosity.

On the other hand, black Americans liked and admired their African sisters' and brothers' sense of dignity and intelligence and their versatility in many social situations. They saw the Africans as "a beautiful people" with a "beautiful culture" which they admired a great deal. They also liked the Africans' beautiful, flowing, colorful costumes.

In Chapter 5 the respondents from both groups indicated that there were social interactions going on among the groups— contrary to the Eurocentric view that there were hardly any social interactions between these groups and if there were any, they were strained.

Hence, in answer to the first set of questions, we find a very healthy and wholesome relationship existing between black Americans and Africans. They do care and identify with one another through their social interactions.

In response to the second set of questions, that is, the investigation into black social strains, the data indicated that black social interactions were oftentimes strained. However, causes that have been seen as contributing directly or indirectly to the strained relationships between black Americans and Africans were based upon such issues as "cultural differences." For instance, differences in mode of dress, habits, foods, mannerisms, and language, do exist. Although differences in social environments and subsequent socialization processes blacks have been born and brought up with in the Old World and in the New are a fact, they do not constitute an unbreachable gap, for most black Americans have retained some of the African cultural characteristics. Black Africans also appreciate some of the black American cultural characteristics such as music and

dance. The long-perceived gap is being slowly bridged as members of both groups attempt to "get themselves together."[6]
Black people have natural affinities: their genealogy, the things they like and admire about one another, and the need to identify with one another.

Chapter 5 indicated that black American and African social interactions are present, while Chapters 6 and 7 also indicated that these two groups also socially interacted with whites to a larger degree than previously suspected. However, strains inherent in the relationships were perceived to come from the Africans' social interactions with whites. The whites have come between the two groups of blacks. Myths and stereotypes, superiority complexes, and ignorance about things African were mentioned as strain-causing agents. The most important point to be noted and emphasized here again is the fact that these strain-causing elements do not come from Africans or their black American counterparts but are perceived as coming from somewhere outside these two groups; they come from whites who are said to have deliberately spawned myths and stereotypes to demean black peoples and to keep them deliberately separated and isolated so they can be dominated. Clearly, whites in general and specifically white females emerged as the "middlemen" who had come between these two black groups as they attempted to get themselves together again.

It is imperative to remember that in important matters that concern black peoples as a group in general, time and time again the black people around the world tend to forget their personal, cultural, or national differences and to line up together. The information about the brutal attack on civil rights workers in Alabama will be long remembered. Various African foreign ministers were in conference in Ethiopia when the news broke. The Nigerian Foreign Minister rose "to denounce racial discrimination in South Africa and the United States," according to *The New York Times*.[7] In the same article, it was reported that "American observers have been dismayed to hear Alabama linked with South Africa in attacks on apartheid inside and outside the conference hall" and, further, that "American corres-

pondents approaching members of the delegations frequently
hear the question, "What's the latest news from Birmingham?"
 The New York Times quoted the Ethiopian Herald, an official publication of the Ministry of Information, as follows:

> What happened in Birmingham last week shows the United
> States in its true light. To be Black is still a crime. . . . The
> colored American must fight hard for freedom rather than
> waste time and much energy bellyaching about Commun-
> ism. The United States' version of "civilized apartheid"
> must be fought.[8]

 The act of concern among the African foreign ministers and
the Ethiopian official communication about Africans' feelings
and concern for their own brothers and sisters did not stop
there. Milton Obote, then Prime Minister of Uganda, was more
than concerned about the Alabama atrocities and took it upon
himself to send a cable to then President John F. Kennedy on
behalf of thirty African nations gathered in Addis Ababa to
protest the "most inhumane treatment against blacks." The
cable read:

> [There is] nothing more paradoxical than that these events
> should take place in the United States at the time when
> that country is anxious to project its image before the
> world as the archetype of democracy and champion of
> freedom.[9]

 At a news conference held on May 23, 1962, as reported in
The New York Times, Prime Minister Obote again lashed out
at the culprits and strongly recognized that those "who had
been doused with blasts of water from fire hoses in Birmingham
were our kith and kin. "The eyes of the world," he added,
"were concentrated on events in Alabama and it is the duty of
the free world, and more so of countries that hold themselves

up as leaders of the free world, to see that all their citizens,
regardless of color, are free."

When racial injustices have been committed against black
people in America by white people, these matters often received front-page coverage in African newspapers and the rest
of the mass media. The African public outcry is almost always
unanimous.

African marches to protest racial injustices in the United
States have been organized and carried out, some peaceful,
others not. In addition, Africans have been known to storm
American embassies abroad to show their moral support for
their brothers and sisters in America. This African concern for
their American counterparts is not one-way. Black Americans
have also indicated the same racial solidarity for their African
sisters and brothers many times, on both theoretical and
practical levels, by supporting liberation movements in Africa
and various protests against colonial powers that still rule parts
of black Africa, as in South Africa.

Most of the difficulties that occur in their social relationships have come, as indicated throughout this study, from the
ways in which black peoples have been defined by predominantly powerful, economic, political, and sociocultural powers
of the world and their structures, the white segment of the
populace. Western cultures have been defined as "civilized,"
the indigenous cultures as "primitive." One has been defined
as "good," "superior," and white, while the other has been
defined as "bad," "inferior," and nonwhite.

However, it has also been discovered that all the black people
are united with each other through the bonds of "ancestry
and that of color." There is also another dimension of unity:
black people are united and find their affinity to each other is
based upon long, common suffering under alien hands—the
chains and yoke of oppression and suppression by predominantly white groups. In Africa where the continent is predominantly black, one finds some new, superficial boundaries
which had been drawn by alien European powers during the
scramble for and demarcation of Africa. Even now, black
Africans often define themselves as "French-speaking,"

"English-speaking," or "Spanish-speaking," rather than identifying with their native African languages.

Blacks in Africa and those scattered throughout the world have another kind of affinity to each other. They are questioning foreign definitions that have been used to label them in the past, definitions that have sometimes seemed alien or inappropriate. They are considering traditional African ways in order to define themselves and their relationships through the concept of "Negritude." They are considering outlooks that differ considerably from traditional Western scientific methods of analysis. They are giving more credence to their inner feelings, to their emotionalism, and to an inner strength that has helped them endure so many hardships.

It has been noted that some differences among black Americans and Africans come from outside the two groups. It is taken for granted that some differences exist, between the groups, symptomatic of the kinds of social strains that are quite normal between groups and individuals. For example, at one time or another, there are strains or quarrels between husband and wife, between parents and their children, between siblings, and others. Despite strains, the close ties persist. This applies also in the case of black American and African relationships. Blacks may have personal differences and quarrels with each other, but this should never be taken to dismiss or discount the important bonds that persist. For deep down inside, blacks all know that they are one people, and this is an important bond. It is a bond that continues to unite black people.

Conclusions Based on Philosophical Orientation
Eurocentric Versus Afrocentric Approach

In conclusion, it is fitting to ask one last, but important, question: Why do people who investigate the same social phenomenon—black American and African identifications with one another—reach different conclusions? It has already been pointed out that this occurs because each premise takes divergent theoretical, as well as methodological conceptualizations. Some scholars give further reasons for these divergent orientations.

Mintz' (1970) discussions concerning field work done said:
"Field work among Afro-Americans was not the way to get
ahead," and in answering the question, "Why not?" he added
that "to those privileged groups studying minority cultures,
it can be embarrassing to defend the values of [the people under
study when they] are members of an oppressed minority, while
the [anthropologist]—like it or not—is a member of the oppressing majority." He continued to stress that "most of us—the
author included—have been far readier to study Afro-American
cultures elsewhere than to study Afro-American cultures in
our own country."[10]

Charles A. Valentine interpreted the views of Gough,
Berreman and Wolfe and Jorgenson by saying:

> Neither liberal ideology nor scientific integrity has stopped
> anthropology from becoming, all too often, either a direct
> instrument of Western imperialism overseas or a passive
> witness of systematic ethnic oppression at home.[11]

Stanley Diamond revealed the following about those with a
Westernized perspective:

> White men have been looking at Negroes . . . for three
> centuries; and they have seen next to nothing . . . yet this
> is a failure, not of experience, but of perception of experi-
> ences for any White man thwarted, seduced, by social
> lies, dangling traditionalless, vocationally misplaced, his
> status in the world denied, his risk in the world meaning-
> less, his masculinity cut off, knows what it is to be a
> Negro, but he doesn't know what he knows.[12]

Valentine did not spare those social scientists with
a Eurocentric perspective on the study of blacks or any other
minority groups, who might otherwise care less about their subjects. He offered a penetrating answer to why they were interested in studying minority groups:

> It helps them to maintain the nonpartisan pose of academic
> or scientific scholarship. By looking only at the ideas or
> beliefs of the dominant group and confining attention to
> supposedly internal customs of the minority, it is possible

to appear objective or neutral on the issues of Black survival and societal change. Yet this is a "neutrality" that supports the status quo, for it never raises problems which might question the fundamental structure of society. This basic assumption that substituting more refined knowledge for crude stereotypes of Afro-Americans will solve Black problems completely ignores the fact that scientific knowledge is frequently used by power holders against the interests of the powerless.[13]

Valentine, a man with a passionate Afrocentric perspective in his studies of black people, noted that often "social scientists seem to express such views most clearly when they are reacting against positions opposed to their own."[14]

One such example Valentine cited is a position taken by William Stewart's reaction to Valentine's paper that questioned the thesis of "Brain Damage or No Father" homes. Stewart is said to have pointed out that he (Stewart) and others "have begun to take seriously the possibility that racists were right in the essence of their facts."[15]

Mead's reaction to Valentine's suggestion that those with Eurocentric views should take a much more participatory research method in attempts to understand blacks and their culture better was more than revealing:

Valentine's plea for participatory research (among poor people, Afro-American or any other) suffers from false premise. The anthropologist who lives with a primitive people adds his respect for their way of life to that of the people he studies. The poverty version of modern culture contains many elements which require repudiation rather than respect; shared repudiation becomes inevitably partisan and requires involvement, an application of anthropology rather than pure research. Where primitive people's dignity is enhanced by objective research, the poor often feel further demeaned.[16]

While Elliot Skinner (1973) went directly to the heart of the matter, he called those with a Westernized view "self-proclaimed . . . specialists." "A number of self-proclaimed White specialists on Africans and Afro-Americans tried to reassure White Americans that there was no real relationship between Afro-Americans and Africa."[17] Assuming that ideally scientific methods are objective and scientists go after scientific truth, it is not clear why the "participatory research method" can gain respect and dignity for a group of people in one situation and "demean" another in a different situation—or why it would require scientific "involvement" in one situation, while in another only a "partisan approach."

If the Eurocentric perspective provides a biased, distorted, mythical, and stereotyped image of blacks, by whom and how can blacks be studied scientifically or otherwise in order to provide a more balanced and truthful study? Those scholars with an Afrocentric perspective have made some suggestions that deserve attention.

The International Conference on African History that met in Dar es Salaam, Tanzania, in 1965, for example, raised issues about the continuity of African history and its role in African development. It was clearly affirmed that: "It is only the African people who through an interpretation and safe-guarding of their history can say what they were, what they are and what they want to be."[18]

Benjamin Quarles stated: "It is impossible for American society to be properly appraised if Blacks are left out of the picture." Columbia historian Walter Metzger emphasized: "We cannot understand America without the help of those studies now called 'Black.' " John W. Blassingame agreed that "no American can truly understand his own society and culture without a knowledge of the roles Negroes have played in them."[19]

J. F. Ade Ajayi and E. J. Alagoa, both outstanding African historians, viewed and defined what they felt should be the role of history within African society:

> . . . to provide a sense of continuity, and to explain to each person and to each people where they fit into the scheme of things. A man's self-perception is vital to what he does and his self-perception is still largely the result of his view of history. If African history is to provide the African with

this self-perception, and thus to play an effective role in independent Africa, it has to correct the distortion and bridge the gap created by the colonial experience in the African historical tradition. African history must evolve its own identity independent of Western historiography, the shackles outside acceptability notwithstanding.[20]

These few examples have not only provided a criticism of the Eurocentric view but also an alternative view suggestive of how to go about studying black relationships.

Importance of Black Study

One of the most important discoveries in this study that must be reemphasized is that those issues that have been applied by the Eurocentric view to point to black Americans' and Africans' lack of identifications have been misplaced. What this study has done has been to place them within their rightful sources. They have come from somewhere outside black Americans and Africans; they have come from whites and others who hold a Eurocentric view of black relationships.

The theoretical implication of the Eurocentric view is a myopic one. It fails to give credit where it is due or to blame the real culprit who has introduced, developed, and perpetuated the social stereotypes that demean and rob other peoples of their dignity and humanity. It has not been the blacks who have perfected "negative" images of themselves. It has been whites, who have come between the two groups and attempted to peddle false stories and, as "middlemen," become cultural brokers of the two groups.

Myths and stereotypes have characterized black peoples as having a "colonial mentality" or a "slave mentality." In their larger implications, these terms are class-based—some blacks are said to harbor "colonial" or "slave" mentalities and have absorbed, assimilated, and want to aspire to the white colonialist's or slave master's way of life rather than their own. Some classical studies that deal with the problems of race

and ethnicity have indicated that the larger American society
is divided into racial groups of whites and nonwhites, as represented in the southern United States as a caste-class system.
Several studies have also pointed out that the black community
is also divided into several social class groupings, each with its
own dominant distinctive "life styles."[21] Miller and Roby
(1970)[22] have dealt with black culture and history with this
point of view in mind.

What emerges from social class studies is the fact that they
all share the idea that each class has its own distinctive "lifestyles," although, as Miller states, for example, others make it
a special point to stress that social patterns may vary within a
class.

The social classifications of blacks into different classes
characterize the upper and middle classes as "respectable" and
"healthy" in their lifestyles, while those in the bottom strata
are characterized as "deviant," "disorganized," and "pathological" in their lifestyles. Since the bulk of the black population are perceived to fall within the bottom social strata, obviously
ly it is to be concluded that black social and cultural life is also
"deviant," "disorganized," and "pathological." What has this
implication of the black social profile done to blacks? The best
answer was that given by Valentine (1971) when he said:

> The effect on Black university students is devastating, as
> they simultaneously strive for a positive identity and
> struggle with their professors' pronouncements that Black
> behavior equals deviance. Not a few Black militants have
> found themselves confronting similar contradictions, as
> when they stress group difference created by class and
> caste oppression and end up portraying themselves as
> carriers of a degraded, deviant life style.[23]

The new generation of black university students feel outraged
by these distorted views of their culture and social behavior.
Unlike their forefathers, they are not trying to be integrated.
As Drake once noted: "Integration, in the final analysis, also
means that the Negro community must increasingly become

more 'middle class' in values and behavior if it is to win respect and approval."[24]

Hence, the myth of superiority/inferiority serves to perpetuate class conflicts among blacks themselves. These are some of the actions and reactions of blacks trying to assert themselves through their diverse developments of common identity. Blacks have found that they have to forge an identity and unity among and between themselves; they have to find common grounds, common denominators on which to base their common identity.

If these theoretical issues have to be realistically understood and studied, then they will have to be placed within their own correct perspectives. By implication, new methodologies have to be devised and applied for their better understanding. Perhaps what is clearly needed is the proper scientific methods of investigation—*verstehen* would be most suitable for such a study. For example, black people must speak for themselves. Autobiographical studies focusing on black peoples in their own historical settings as well as examinations into the effects of political, economic, and social conditions of the time must be made. The psychological implications that shape and influence such people's feelings and their thinking and views about themselves, others, and the world at large are important. "Black experience" should and can best be studied and interpreted by black scholars or those who use an Afrocentric perspective.

In a wider perspective, though they are not necessarily comparable, cross-cultural studies concerning other ethnic groups in America and their ancestral origins elsewhere should be carried out in order to give blacks a better, wider understanding and a broader range for comparative purposes. This will provide a more global interpretation of the extent and nature of such relationships that exist between peoples of the New World and those from the Old—Europe, Africa, Latin America, and Asia.

This study, therefore, has attempted and hopefully succeeded in its contribution to our knowledge of the relationships between black Americans and Africans. Past studies concerning black Americans' and Africans' social relationships have, by and large, concentrated on only one of the aspects of social situations, placing major emphasis on "strains" rather than on "harmony," on "differences" rather than "similarities." Often these myopic views lead them to focus on black peoples' supposedly strained social relationships rather than viewing the problem in the proper perspective. As this study has revealed, black strains are engendered outside of black sources.

Hence, this study has provided a more balanced look at the social relationships between black Americans and Africans. It has provided a new perspective. That is, by examining these relationships for both positive and negative aspects, it has added a new perspective in which, hopefully, future studies can be based. Without over-stressing the importance of this study, because of its exploratory nature, it is firmly believed that some initial ground has been broken in which to lay the foundations for future, more refined research concerning black Americans' and Africans' social relationships. And finally, it is hoped that this study will stimulate interest for further social scientific inquiry in this important, but long-neglected, area.

Notes

1. Nathan Glazer and Daniel Patrick Moynihan, *Beyond the Melting Pot* (Cambridge, Mass.: M.I.T. and Harvard University Press, 1963); E. Franklin Frazier, *The Negro Family in the United States* (Chicago: The University of Chicago Press, 1966); Kenneth M. Stampp, *The Peculiar Institution: Slavery in the AnteBellum South* (New York: Alfred A. Knopf, 1956).

2. Glazer and Moynihan, *Beyond the Melting Pot*; Frazier, 1966; Thorsten Sellin, *Culture, Conflict, and Crime* (New York: Social Science Research Council, 1938); George B. Vold, *Theoretical Criminology* (New York: Oxford University Press, 1958); Richard Quinney, *The Social Reality of Crime* (Boston: Little, Brown, 1970).

3. For example, see John A. Davis (ed.), *Africans Seen by American Negroes* (New York: American Society of African Culture, 1958); John A. Davis, R. D. Hanson, and D. R. Burnor, *IIE Survey of the African Student: His Achievements and His Problems* (New York: International Institute of Education, 1961); Harold R. Isaacs, "The American Negro and Africa:

Some Notes," *Phylon* 20 (Fall, 1959); and Jane W. Jacqz, *African Students at U.S. Universities* (New York: African Institute [AAI], 1967).

4. For example, see Melville J. Herskovits, *The Myth of the Negro Past* (New York: Harper and Brothers, 1941); W. E. B. Du Bois, *The World and Africa* (New York: International Publishers, 1946); Charles A. Valentine, *Black Studies and Anthropology: Scholarly and Political Interest in Afro-American Culture* (Addison-Wesley Modular Publication 15, 1972).

5. For example, see Elliot P. Skinner, *Afro-Americans and Africa: The Continuing Dialectic* (New York: Columbia University, 1972).

6. Alex Poinsett, "Festac '77: Cultural Events Draw 17,000 to Lagos." In *Ebony*, 32, 7 (May 1977).

7. *The New York Times*, May 19, 1962.

8. Ibid.

9. *The New York Times*, May 23, 1962.

10. Sidney W. Mintz, "Forward." In *Afro-American Anthropology: Contemporary Perspectives*, Norman E. Whitten and John F. Szwed (eds.), (New York: Macmillan, 1970), pp. 13-14.

11. Charles A. Valentine, *Black Studies and Anthropology: Scholarly and Political Interests in Afro-American Culture*. In *Module* 15 (Reading, Mass.: Addison-Wesley Publishing Co., 1972), p. 28.

12. Stanley Diamond, "The Great Black Hope." In *Black America*, ed. John F. Szwed (New York: Basic Books, 1970), p. 171.

13. Valentine, "Black Studies and Anthropology," p. 24.

14. Ibid., p. 24.

15. Ibid., p. 25.

16. Ibid.

17. Elliot P. Skinner, *Afro-Americans and Africa: The Continuing Dialectic: A Minority Report* (New York: Columbia University, a publication of the Urban Center, 1973), p. 19.

18. T. O. Ranger, ed., *Emerging Themes of African History: Proceedings of the International Congress of African Historians Held at University College, Dar-es-Salaam, October, 1965* (London: 1958).

19. Benjamin Quarles, "Black History Unbound," *Daedalus* 103, no. 2 (Spring 1974): 164.

20. J. F. Ade Ajayi and E. J. Alagoa, "Black Africa: The Historians' Perspective," *Daedalus* 103, no. 2 (Spring 1974): 131.

21. W. Lloyd Warner and Allison Davis, "A Comparative Study of American Caste." In *Race Relations and the Race Problem*, ed. Edgar Thompson (Durham, N.C.: Duke University Press, 1939); Allison Davis

et al., *Deep South* (Chicago: University of Chicago Press, 1941); and John Dollard, *Caste and Class in a Southern Town* (New Haven, Conn.: Yale University Press, 1937).

22. S. M. Miller and Pamela Roby, *The Future of Inequality* (New York: Basic Books, 1970), p. 174.

23. Charles A. Valentine, *Black Studies and Anthropology: Scholarly and Political Interests in Afro-American Culture* (Reading, Pa.: Addison-Wesley Modular Publication, 15, 1972), p. 12.

24. St. Clair Drake, "The Social and Economic Status of the Negro in the United States." In *The Negro American*, ed. Talcott Parsons and Kenneth B. Clark (Boston: Houghton-Mifflin, 1966), p. 36.

Bibliography

Addison, Gayle, Jr., ed. *The Black Aesthetic.* New York: Doubleday and Company, Inc., 1971.

African Heritage Studies Association. Schomburg Collection, New York Public Library, 1969.

Ajayi, J. F. Ade. "The Place of African History and Culture in the Process of Nation Building in Africa South of Sahara." *Journal of Negro Education* 30 (1960).

Ajayi, J. F. Ade, and Alagoa, E. J. "Black Africa: The Historians' Perspective." *Daedalus* 103, 2 (Spring 1974).

Alexander, Pace Rae, and Lester, Julius. *Young and Black in America.* New York: Random House, 1970.

Allen, Samuel. "Negritude: Agreement and Disagreement." Paper presented at the Third Annual AMSAC Conference, New York, June, 1960.

American Negro Leadership Conference on Africa, Resolutions. New York: Harriman, November 23-25, 1962.

Amsterdam News. September 14, 1927.

Apter, David E. *Ghana in Transition.* New York: Athenaeum, 1963.

Aptheker, Herbert. "Consciousness of Negro Nationality: An Historical Survey." *Political Affairs* 27 (June 1949).

———. "Consciousness of Negro Nationality to 1900." *Toward Negro Freedom.* New York: 1956.

Aron, Birgit. "The Garvey Movement: Shadow and Substance." *Phylon* (4th Quarter 1947).

Baldwin, James. *Notes of a Native Son.* Boston: Beacon Press, Inc., 1957.

Ballard, Allen B. *The Education of Black Folk.* New York: Harper and Row, 1973.

Bantom, M. *West African City.* London: Oxford University Press, 1957.
——. "A Negro Essays the Negro Mood." *The New York Times Magazine.* March 12, 1961.
Barbour, Floyd., ed. *The Black Power Revolt.* Boston, Mass.: Porter Sargent, 1968.
Becker, Howard S. "A Note on Interviewing Tactics." *Human Organization* 2 (Winter 1954).
Belewa, T. "Nigeria Looks Ahead." *Foreign Affairs* 41 (October 1962).
Bell, Howard. *Search for a Place: Black Separatism and Africa.* Ann Arbor: University of Michigan Press, 1969.
Billingsley, Andrew. *Black Families in White America.* Englewood Cliffs, N.J.: Prentice-Hall, 1968.
The Black Bulletin. Schomburg Collection. New York Public Library, n.d.
Blackwell, James E. *Black Community: Diversity and Unity.* New York:
Blauner, Robert. "Black Culture: Myth or Reality." *Americans from Africa.* Edited by Peter I. Rose. New York: Atherton, 1969.
Blyden, Edward W. "The African Problem." *North American Review* 141 (September 1895): 327-39.
Bohannan, Paul. *Africa and Africans.* New York: Natural History Press, 1964.
Bourguinon, Erika E. "Religious Synchretism Among New World Negroes." *Afro-American Anthropology: Contemporary Perspectives.* Norman E. Whitten and John F. Szwed, eds. New York: Macmillan, 1970a.
——. "Ritual Dissociation and Possession Belief in Caribbean Negro Religion." *Afro-American Anthropology: Contemporary Perspectives.* Norman E. Whitten and John F. Szwed, eds. New York: Macmillan, 1970b.
Briefman, George., ed. *Malcolm X Speaks.* New York: Merit Publishers, 1965.
Bristed, John. *America and Her Resources.* London: H. Colburn, 1818.
Broderick, Francis L. *W. E. B. Du Bois: Negro Leader in Time of Crisis.* Stanford, Calif.: Stanford University Press, 1959.
Buell, Raymond Leslie. *The Native Problem in Africa.* Vol. 2. New York: Archon Books, 1927.
Carmichael, Stokely, and Hamilton, Charles. *Black Power: The Politics of Liberation in America.* New York: Vintage Books, 1968.
Cartey, Wilfred, and Kilson, Martin. *The African Reader.* New York: Vintage Press, 1970.
Césaire, Aimé. *The Journal Tropique* 2, Forte-de-France, Martinque (July 1941).

The Chicago Bee. "Pan-African Congress Public Manifesto." September 3, 1927. Schomburg Collection. New York Public Library.

Clarke, John Henrik. "The Search for Africa." *Negro Digest* 17 (February 1968): 29.

——. "The New Afro-American Nationalism." *Freedomways* 1 (Fall 1961): 285-95.

——, ed. *Harlem, U.S.A.* Berlin: Seven Seas Publishers, 1964.

Cleaver, Eldridge. *Post-Prison Writings and Speeches.* New York: Random House, 1968.

——. *Soul on Ice.* New York: Dell, 1968.

——. *On Ideology of the Black Panther Party.* San Francisco: Black Panther Party, 1970.

Cohen, Robert D. "African Students and the Negro-American Past Relationships and Recent Program." *International and Cultural Exchange* 5 (Fall 1969): 76-85.

Coleman, James. "Nationalism in Tropical Africa." *American Political Science Review* 67 (1954).

Cook, Mercer. "The Aspirations of Negritude." *New Leader* 43 (October 24, 1960): 8-10.

Couch, William, Jr., ed. *New Black Playwrights: An Anthology.* Baton Rouge: Louisiana State University Press, 1968.

Crocker, W. R. *Nigeria: A Critique of British Colonial Administration.* London: George Allen Unwin, Ltd., 1936.

Cronon, Edmund David. *Black Moses, the Story of Marcus Garvey and The Universal Negro Improvement Association.* Madison, Wis.: The University of Michigan Press, 1964.

Crooks, J. J. *A History of the Colony of Sierra Leone, West Africa.* Dublin: Metro Books, 1903.

Crowley, Daniel J. "African Folktales in Afro-American." *Black America.* Edited by John F. Szwed. New York: Basic Books, 1970.

Cruse, Harold W. "Negro Nationalism's New Wave." *New Leader* 35 (March 19, 1962).

——. "Revolutionary Nationalism and the Afro-American." *Studies on the Left* 2 (1962).

——. "An Afro-American's Cultural Views." *Presence Africaine* 10 (December 1957-January 1958).

——. *The Crisis of the Negro Intellectual from Its Origins to the Present.* New York: William Morrow and Company, Inc., 1967.

——. "Racial Integration and Negritude: A Philosophical View." A paper presented at the Third Annual Conference, American Society of African Culture, 1960.

Crutcher, John. "Pan-Africanism: African Odyssey." *Current History* 44 (January 1963).

Curtin, Philip D. *The Image of Africa: British Ideas and Actions, 1780-1850.* Madison, Wis.: The University of Wisconsin Press, 1964.

Davis, John A., ed. *Africans Seen by American Negroes.* New York: American Society of African Culture, 1958.

Davis, John, Hanson, R., and Burnor, D. *II E Survey of the African Student: His Achievements and His Problems.* New York: Institute of International Education, 1961.

DeFleur, Melvin C., D'Antonio, William V., and DeFleur, Louis. *Sociology: Man and Society.* Glenview, Ill.: Scott, Foresman and Co., 1971.

Degler, Carl N. "The Negro in America—Where Myrdal Went Wrong." *New York Times Magazine,* December 7, 1969.

Dennis, Ethel R. *The Black People of America.* New York: McGraw Hill Book Co., 1970.

Diamond, Stanley. "The Great Black Hope." *Black-America.* Edited by John F. Szwed. New York: Basic Books, 1970.

Diop, Alioune. Opening Address to First Congress of Negro Writers and Artists, Paris. *Presence Africaine,* Nos. 8, 9, 10 (1957-58).

Dollard, John. *Caste and Class in a Southern Town.* New Haven, Conn.: Yale University Press, 1937.

Donnan, Elizabeth. *Documents Illustrative on the Slave Trade to America. II-IV.* Washington, D.C.: Octagon: 1930-1935.

Drake, St. Clair. "Pan-Africanism, What It Is." *Africa Today* 14 (January-February 1959): 6-11.

Drake, St. Clair, and Cayton, Horace R. *Black Metropolis, A Study of Negro Life in a Northern City.* New York: Harper and Row, 1945.

Drake, St. Clair. "The Social and Economic Status of the Negro in the United States." *The Negro American.* Edited by Talcott Parsons and Kenneth B. Clark. Boston: Houghton-Mifflin, 1966.

——. *Negritude and Soul: Reflections out of Africa.* Atlanta, Ga.: Institute of the Black World, 1970.

——. *The Redemption of Africa and Black Religion.* Chicago, Ill.: The Third World Press, 1970.

Drake, St. Clair, and Cayton, Horace R. *Black Metropolis, A Study of Negro Life in a Northern City.* New York: Harper and Row, 1945.

Du Bois, W. E. B. *The Souls of Black Folk: Essays and Sketches.* Chicago: A. C. McLurg and Co., 1903.

——. *Black Reconstruction.* New York: Harcourt Brace, 1935.

——. *The World and Africa.* New York: International Publishers, 1946.

——. *Dusk and Dawn: An Essay Toward an Autobiography of a Race Concept.* New York: Harcourt Brace & Co., 1940.

Duncan, John M. *Travels Through Part of the United States and Canada in 1818 and 1819.* New York: Frank Cass Ltd. (International School Book Service), 1823.

Ellison, Ralph. *Shadow and Act.* New York: Random House, 1964.

Essien-Udom, E. E. *Black Nationalism: A Search for Identity in America.* Chicago: University of Chicago Press, 1962.

——. "The Nationalist Movements in Harlem." *Freedomways* 2 (Summer 1963): 335-342.

Fanon, Frantz. *Black Skin, White Mask.* New York: Grove Press, Inc., 1967.

——. *The Wretched of the Earth.* New York: Grove Press, Inc., 1965.

——. *Toward the African Revolution.* New York: Grove Press, Inc., 1968.

——. *A Dying Colonialism.* New York: Grove Press, Inc., 1967.

Ferris, William H. *An African Abroad and His Evolution in Western Civilization.* New York: New Harlem, 1936.

Fisher, Miles Mark. "Deep River." *Black Brotherhood: Afro-Americans and Africa.* Edited by Uya Edet Okon. Lexington, Mass.: D. C. Heath & Co., 1971.

Foote, Andrew Hull. *Africa and the American Flag.* New York: Beekman Publishers, 1854.

Franklin, John Hope. *From Slavery to Freedom: History of Negro Americans.* 3rd ed. New York: Alfred A. Knopf, Inc., 1948.

Frazier, E. Franklin. *Negro Youth at the Crossways: Personality Development in the Middle States.* Washington, D.C.: American Council on Education, 1940.

——. *The Negro Family in the United States.* Chicago: The University of Chicago Press, 1966.

——. *Black Bourgeoisie.* New York: Collier Books, 1962.

Fuller, Hoyt W. *Journey to Africa.* Chicago: The Third World Press, 1971.

Fulwinder, P. S. *The Mind and Mood of Black America.* New York: Dorsey Press, 1969.

Garrison, Lloyd. *Thoughts on African Colonizations: Or an Impartial Exhibition of the Doctrine and Purposes of the American Colonization Society.* Boston, Mass.: Garrison and Knopp, 1832.

Garvey, Marcus. *Philosophy and Opinions of Marcus Garvey.* New York: Universal Publishing House, 1923.

Gayle, Addison, Jr., ed. *The Black Aesthetic.* New York: Doubleday and Company, Inc., 1971.

Geis, Gilbert, and Bittle, William. *The Longest Way Home: Chief Alfred Sam's Back to Africa Movement.* Detroit: Wayne State University Press, 1964.

Genovese, Eugene D. "The Legacy of Slavery and the Roots of Black Nationalism." *Studies on the Left* 6 (November-December 1966): 3-26.

Glazer, Nathan, and Moynihan, Daniel Patrick. *Beyond the Melting Pot.* Cambridge, Mass.: M.I.T. and Harvard University Press, 1963.

Goldthorpe, J. E. "Educated Africans: Some Conceptual and Terminological Problems." *Social Change in Modern Africa.* Edited by Aidan Southall. London: Oxford University Press, 1961.

Green, A. H. M. "American in the Niger Valley: A Colonization Centennary." *Phylon* 20: 225-239.

Gregor, James A. "Black Nationalism: A Preliminary Analysis of Negro Radicalism." *Science and Society* 28 (Fall 1963).

Gutman, Herbert C. *The Black Family in Slavery and Freedom 1750-1925.* New York: Pantheon Books, 1976.

Halston, John. *Black Africans and Black-Americans on an American Campus: The African View.* Unpublished paper, Los Angeles: University of California at Los Angeles, 1968.

Hapgood, David. "The Competition for Africa's Students." *The Reporter* (September 12, 1963): 41-42.

Harding, Vincent. "Beyond Chaos: Black History and the Search for the New Land." *Amistad.* Edited by John A. Williams and Charles F. Harris. New York: Random House, 1970.

Hare, Nathan. "A Radical Perspective on Social Science Curricula." *Black Studies in the University: A Symposium.* Edited by Armstead L. Robinson, et al. New Haven, Conn.: Yale University Press, 1969.

Harrington, Michael. *The Other America: Poverty in the United States.* New York: Macmillan, 1962.

Haynes, George Edmund. "Americans Look at Africa." *Journal of Negro Education* 26 (Winter 1958): 94-100.

——. *The Anthropometry of the American Negro.* New York: Columbia University Press, 1930.

Herskovits, Melville J. "What Has Africa Given America?" *New Republic.* No. 1083 (1935b): 92-96.

——. *The Myth of the Negro Past.* New York: Harper and Brothers, 1941.

——. "The Present Status and Needs of Afro-American Research." *The New World Negro.* Edited by F. S. Herskovits. Bloomington: Indiana University Press, 1966.

Hill, Adelaid C., and Kilson, Martin. *Apropos of Africa*. London: Frank
Cass and Co., Ltd., 1969.

Hill, Herbert, ed. *Soon One Morning: New Writings by American Negroes.
1940-1962*. New York: Knopf, 1963.

Hodgkins, T., and Schachter, Ruth. *French-Speaking West Africa in
Transition: International Conciliation*. New York: Carnegie Endow-
ment for International Peace, 1960.

Hughes, Anthony J. "Interview with Randall Robinson, Executive Director, Transafrica." In *Africa Report* 25, 1 New York: The African
American Institute (January-February 1980).

Hughes, Langston. *The Weary Blues*. New York: Dodd, Mead, 1926.

———. *The Book of Negro Folklore*. New York: Dodd, Mead, 1959.

Isaacs, Harold R. "Western Man and the African Crisis." *Saturday Review*
36 (May 2, 1953): 11.

———. "The American Negro and Africa: Some Notes." *Phylon* 20 (Fall
1959).

———. *Emergent Americans: A Report on Crossroads Africa*. New York:
Viking Press, 1961.

———. "Back to Africa." *The New Yorker* 36 (May 13, 1961).

———. *The New World of Negro Americans*. New York: The John Day
Company, 1963.

Jackson, Jackquelyne J. "But Where Are the Men." *The Black Scholar*
(December 1976).

Jacqz, Jane W. *African Students at U.S. Universities*. New York: African-
American Institute (AAI), 1967.

Jahn, Jahneinz. *Muntu: The New African Culture*. New York: Grove
Press, Inc., 1961.

———. *Neo-African Literature: A History of Black Writing*. New York:
Grove Press, Inc., 1968.

James, C. L. R. *A History of Pan-African Revolt*. Washington, D.C.: Drum
and Spear Press, 1969.

Jones, LeRoi. *Blues People: The Negro Experience in White America and
the Music That Developed from It*. New York: William Morrow and
Company, 1963.

Kennedy, Joseph C. "The American Negro's Key Role In Africa." *The
New York Times Magazine* (February 4, 1962): 27.

Kent, George. *Blackness and the Adventure of Western Culture*. Chicago,
Ill.: Third World Press, 1971.

Kenyatta, Jomo. *Facing Mount Kenya*. New York: Vintage Press, 1938.

Killian, Lewis M. *The Impossible Revolution? Black Power and the
American Dream*. New York: Random House, 1968.

Kwayana, Eusi. "Brothers and Sisters." *Pan-African Secretariat* (April
1971).

Legum, Colin. *Pan-Africanism.* London: Pall Mall Press, 1962.
——. *Pan-Africanism—A Short Political Guide.* New York: F. A. Praeger, 1961.
Levin, Harry. *The Power of Blackness.* New York: Grove Press, 1958.
Lewis, Frances E. *Guardian.* August 27, 1924.
Liebow, Elliot. *Tally's Corner: A Study of Negro Street-Corner Men.* Boston: Little, Brown, 1967.
Lincoln, Eric. "Mood Ebony: The Acceptance of Being Black." *American from Africa: Old Memories, New Moods.* Edited by Peter I. Rose. New York: Atherton Press, Inc., 1970.
Livingston, John. "The African Student in the United States." *Africa As Seen by American Negroes.* Edited by John A. Davis. New York: American Society of African Culture, 1958.
Locke, Alain. *The New Negro.* New York: Atheneum Edition, 1968.
Locke, Alain, et al., eds. *The New Negro: An Interpretation.* New York: Albert and Charles Boni, 1925.
Logan, Rayford. "The American Negro's View of Africa." *Africa As Seen by American Negroes.* Edited by John A. Davis. New York: American Society of African Culture, 1958.
Logan, W. F. *The Betrayal of the Negro.* New York: Macmillan Co., 1965.
Lomay, Alan. "The Homogeneity of Afro-American Musical Style." *Afro-American Anthropology: Contemporary Perspectives.* Edited by Norman E. Whitten and John F. Szwed, New York: Macmillan, 1970.
Lomax, Alan. "The Homogeneity of Afro-American Musical Style."
Lomax, Louis E. *The Negro Revolt.* New York: Harper and Row, 1926.
Lynch, Hollis. *Edward Wilmont Blyden: Pan-Negro Patriot 1832-1912.* New York: Oxford University Press, 1970.
——. "Pan-Negro Nationalism in the New World, Before 1862." *African History,* Vol. 2. Edited by Jeffrey Buhle. Boston: Boston University Press, 1966.
Maglangbayan. *Garvey, Lumumba, Malcolm: Black Nationalist-Separatists.* Chicago, Ill.: Third World Press, 1971.
Magubane, George Bernard. *Ideology of Pride and Prejudice: Afro-Americans' Conception of Africans.* New York: NOK Publishers, 1974.
Marx, Gary T. "The Social Context of Militancy." *Protest and Prejudice.* New York: Harper and Row, 1967, pp. 47-49.
Mboya, Joseph Thomas. *Freedom and After.* London: Brown and Co., 1963.
McKay, Claude. *Harlem: Negro Metropolis.* New York: E. P. Dutton & Co., 1940.
McWorter, Gerald. "The Ideology of Black Social Science." *The Black Scholar* (December 1969).

Mehlinger, Louis R. "The Attitude of the Free Negro Toward African Colonization." *Journal of Negro History* 1 (July 1916): 271-201.

Merril, Francis E. *Society and Culture.* Englewood Cliffs, New Jersey: Prentice-Hall, Inc., 1969.

Miller, S. M., and Roby, Pamela. *The Future of Inequality.* New York: Basic Books, 1970.

Mintz, Sidney W. "Forward." *Afro-American Anthropology: Contemporary Perspectives.* Edited by Norman E. Whitten and John F. Szwed. New York: Macmillan, 1970.

Moore, Richard B. *The Name "negro": Its Origins and Its Evil Use.* New York: Afroamerican Publisher 1960.

——. "Du Bois and Pan-Africa." *Black Brotherhood: Afro-Americans and Africa.* Edited by Uya Edet Ukon. Lexington, Mass.: D. C. Heath and Co., 1971.

——. "Africa Conscious Harlem." *American from Africa: Old Memories, New Moods.* Edited by Peter I. Rose. New York: Atherton Press, Inc. 1970.

Morris, Richard T. *The Two-Way Mirror: National Status in Foreign Student's Adjustment.* Minneapolis: University of Minnesota Press, 1960.

Mphahlele, Ezekiel. *The African Image.* New York: Praeger, 1962.

Myrdal, Gunnar. *An American Dilemma: The Negro Problem and Modern Democracy.* New York: Harper and Brothers, 1944.

Nesbit, Robert A. *The Social Bond: An Introduction to the Study of Society.* New York: Alfred A. Knopf, Inc., 1970.

Newsweek. September 4, 1972.

New York Amsterdam News. August 24, 1924.

——. September 14, 1927.

New York Post. "Negroes Demand Racial Equality." November 19, 1921.

New York Times. May 19, 1967.

——. May 24, 1963.

Nigerian High Commission. *The Future of Pan-Africanism.* London: Nigerian High Commission, 1961.

Nkrumah, Kwame. *Consciencism: Philosophy and Ideology for Decolonialization and Development with Particular Reference to the African Revolution.* Hememan, London, 1964.

——. *The African Background Outlined: Handbook for the Study of the Negro.* Washington, D.C.: The Association for the Study of Negro Life and History, Inc., 1936.

——. *African Heroes and Heroines.* Washington, D.C.: The Associated Publishers, Inc., 1939.

——. *Africa Must Unite*. London: International Publishing Co., 1963.
——. *I Speak of Freedom: A Statement of African Ideology*. New York: Praeger, 1961.
Ojigbo, Okion A. *Young and Black in Africa*. New York: Random House, 1971.
Okoye, Mukwunyo. *African Responses*. Bristol: Arthur H. Stockwell Ltd., 1964.
Olympio, Sylvanus. "African Problems and the Cold War." *Foreign Affairs* 40 (October 1961).
Ottley, Roy. *New World A'Coming*. Boston: Houghton Mifflin Co., 1943.
Ovington, Mary. *Portraits of Colour*. New York: Viking, 1927.
Padmore, George. *Pan-Africanism or Communism?* New York: Rory Publishers, 1956.
——. *Colonial and Coloured Unity, Program of Action. History of the Pan-African Congress*. Hammersmith, London, 1963.
Pan-African Congress. *Bulletin I*. Compiled by Public Committee Circle for Peace and Foreign Relations, August 21, 1927.
Pan-African Congress Public Manifesto. *Chicago Bee*. September 3, 1927.
Poinsett, Alex. "Festac '77: Festival in Nigeria Strengthens Bond Between Black-America and Africa." *Ebony* 32, 7 (May 1977).
Quarles, Benjamin. "Black History Unbound." *Daedalus* 103, 2 (Spring 1974): 164.
Ranger, T. O., ed. *Emerging Themes of African History*. Proceedings of the International Congress of African Historians held at University College. Dar-es-Salaam (October 1965).
Record, Wilson. "The Negro Intellectual and Negro Nationalism." *Social Forces* 33 (October 1954-May 1955).
——. "Extremist Movements Among American Negroes." *Phylon* (1st Quarter 1956).
Redkey, Edwin. *Black Exodus: Black Nationalist and Back to Africa Movements 1890-1910*. New Haven, Conn.: Yale University Press, 1969.
Reid, Ira D. *The Negro Immigrant: His Background, Characteristics and Social Adjustment, 1899-1937*. New York: Arno Press, 1969.
Report of the National Advisory Commission on Civil Disorders. New York: Bantam Books, 1968.
Robeson, Paul. *Here I Stand*. New York: Othello Associates, 1958.
Robinson, Alma. Sixth Pan-African Conference: Africa and Afro-American." In *Africa Report* 19, 5. New York: The African-American Institute (September-October 1974).
Rolston, Richard D. "A Second Middle Passage: African Student Sojourns

in the United States During the Colonial Period and Their Influences Upon the Character of African Leadership." Ph.D. dissertation, University of California, 1972.

Rose, Peter I. *Americans from Africa: Old Memories, New Moods.* New York: Atherton Press, Inc., 1970.

Royce, Josiah. *Race Questions, Provincialism and Other American Problems.* New York: Books for Libraries, Inc., 1908.

Rubadiri, David. "Why African Literature?" *Transition* 4, 15 (Kampala, 1964).

Sellitz, Claire, Christ, June R., Havel, Joan, and Cook, Stuart W. *Attitudes and Social Relations of Foreign Students in the United States.* Minneapolis: University of Minnesota, 1963.

Senghor, Leopold. "West Africa in Evolution." *Foreign Affairs* 39 (January 1961).

Sewell, Thomas. *Black Education: Myths and Tragedies.* New York: David McKay Co., 1972.

Shepperson, George. "Notes on Negro American Influences on the Emergence of African Nationalism." *Journal of African History* 1 (1960): 299-312.

——, and Price, Thomas. *Independent Africa—John Chilembwe and the Origins, Setting, and Significance of the Nyasaland Native Rising of 1951.* Edinburgh: Thomas Nelison, 1958.

Sierra Leone Company. "Substance of the Report Delivered by the Court of Directors of the Sierra Leone Company to the General Court of Proprietors on Thursday, March 27, 1794." Philadelphia, 1795. George Shepperson unpublished papers, Library of Cong.

Silberman, Charles E. *Crisis in Black and White.* New York: Random House, 1964.

Singleton, F. Seth, and Shingler, John. *Africa in Perspective.* New York: Hayden Book Co., Inc., 1967.

Skinner, Elliot P. *Afro-Americans and Africa: The Continuing Dialectic.* New York: Columbia University, 1973.

Smith, Arthur L. *Language, Communication, and Rhetoric in Black America.* New York: Harper and Row Publishers, 1972.

Stammp, Kenneth M. *The Peculiar Institution: Slavery in the Ante-Bellum South.* New York: Alfred A. Knopf, 1956.

Stone, Eddie. *Andrew Young: Biography of a Realist.* Los Angeles, Calif.: Holloway House Publishing Co., 1980.

Szwed, John F. "Afro-American Musical Adaptation." *Afro-American Anthropology: Contemporary Perspectives.* Edited by Norman E. Whitten and John F. Szwed. New York: Macmillan, 1970.

Thornbrough, Emma L., ed. *Booker T. Washington*. Englewood Cliffs, N.J.: Prentice Hall, 1969.

Thorpe, Earl E. "Africa in the Thought of Negro Americans." *Negro History Bulletin* (October 1959), p. 5.

Touré, Sékou. Quoted in Legum, Colin. *Pan-Africanism: A Short Political Guide*. London: Pall Mall Press, 1962.

Turner, Bishop Henry McNeal. "The American Negro and the Fatherland." *Addresses and Proceedings of the Congress on Africa*, December 13-15, 1895.

Turner, Lorenzo D. "African Survivals in the New World with Special Emphasis on the Arts." *Africa Seen by American Negroes*. Edited by John A. Davis. New York: American Society of African Culture, 1958.

Touré, Sékou. Quoted in Legum, Colin. *Pan-Africanism: A Short Political Guide*. London: Pall Mall Press, 1962.

Stone, Eddie. *Andrew Young: Biography of a Realist*. Los Angeles, Calif.: Holloway House Publishing Co., 1980.

U.S. Advisory Commission on International Educational and Cultural Affairs. *Foreign Students in the United States: A National Survey*. Mimeographed. Washington, D.C., 1966.

Uya, Edet Ukon. *Black Brotherhood: Afro-Americans and Africans*. Lexington, Mass.: D. C. Heath and Company, 1971.

Valentine, Charles A. *Culture and Poverty: Critique and Counter-Proposals*. Chicago: University of Chicago Press, 1968.

———. *Black Studies and Anthropology: Scholarly and Political Interests in Afro-American Culture*, Addison-Wesley Modular Publications 15 (1972).

Veroff, Joseph. "African Students in the United States." *Journal of Social Issues* 19 (July 1963): 48-66.

Walker, David. *One Continual Cry: David Walker's Appeal to the Coloured Citizens of the World (1929-1930)*. New York: Humanities Press, 1965.

Warner, W. Lloyd, and Davis, Allison. "A Comparative Study of American Caste." *Race Relations and the Race Problems*. Edited by Edgar Thompson. Durham, N.C.: Duke University Press, 1939.

Washington, Booker T. *The Future of the American Negro*. Boston: Metro Books, 1899.

Weekly Anglo African. n.p., September 24, 1859.

———. October 1, 1859.

Whitten, Norman E. "Personal Networks and Musical Contexts in the Pacific Lowlands of Columbia and Ecuador." *Afro-American Anthropology: Contemporary Perspectives*. Edited by Norman E. Whitten and John F. Szwed. New York: Macmillan, 1970.

Whitten, Norman E., and Szwed, John F., eds. *Afro-American Anthropology: Contemporary Perspectives.* New York: Macmillan, 1970.

Williams, Eric. *Capitalism and Slavery.* Chapel Hill: University of Carolina Press, 1944.

Wilson, Ernest J. *A Survey of Attitudes and Interests of Foreign Students at Howard University.* Washington, D.C.: Howard University Press, 1965.

Wirth, Louis, and Goldhamer, Herbert. "The Hybrid and the Problem of Miscegenation." *Characteristics of the American Negro.* Edited by Otto Klineberg. New York: n.p., 1944.

Woodis, Jack. *Africa: The Roots of Revolt.* New York: The Citadel Press, 1962.

Woodson, Carter G. *The African Background Outlined or Handbook for the Study of the Negro.* Washington, D.C.: Association Press, 1936.

Woolf, Leonard. *Empire and Commerce in Africa: A Study in Economic Imperialism.* New York: Howard Fertig, Inc., 1968.

Wright, Nathan, Jr. "The Crisis Which Bred Black Power." *The Black Power Revolt.* Edited by Floyd Barbour. Boston: Porter Sargent, 1968, pp. 103-118.

Wright, Richard. *Native Son.* New York: Grosset and Dunlap, 1940.

——. *White Man, Listen!* New York: Doubleday, 1957.

——. "Blueprint for Negro Literature." *Amistad 2.* Edited by John A. Williams and Charles F. Harris. New York: Random House, 1971.

X, Malcolm. *Malcolm X Speaks.* Edited by George Breitman. New York: Merit Publishers, 1965.

——. *The Autobiography of Malcolm X.* New York: Ballantine Press, 1977.

Index

ABOUT THE AUTHOR

JOSEPHINE MORAA MOIKOBU was born in Kenya and educated in
the United States. She is Director of the Office for International Education at the New Jersey State Department of Education.

DATE DUE
